THE ROAD TO GOLGOTHA

The road to Golgotha

The chronology
of the life
of Jesus of Nazareth

Stephen J Dudley

Lasse
Press

First published 2013
by the Lasse Press
2 St Giles Terrace, Norwich NR2 1NS, UK
www.lassepress.com
lassepress@gmail.com

Also published in electronic versions

ISBN-13: 978-0-9568758-5-3

Designed and typeset in IT Baskerville
by Curran Publishing Services Ltd, Norwich, UK

Printed and bound by CPI Group (UK) Ltd, Croydon, CR0 4YY

Front cover illustration: stained glass from the church of
Saint-Pierre, Dreux, France

Contents

Acknowledgements

The research for, and the writing of, this book has taken up an inordinate amount of my time, spread over an embarrassingly large number of years. Now that it is done I can only say thank you to my long-suffering wife Hilary for her patience, tolerance and forbearance, in allowing me to finish what had become something of a personal obsession. To her I must also promise to pay attention now to a few of those aspects of normal life that I may have neglected in the process.

I have also to thank Paul Cooney, who has been a friend for over twenty years, and who was the first person to read what was a very early draft of my investigation. It was he who persuaded me that what I was writing deserved a wider audience, and without his encouragement I doubt that I would ever have considered looking for a publisher.

To Susan Curran I must extend my gratitude for agreeing to edit and publish the product of my endeavours, and for humanely guiding me into reorganizing and rewriting what had been, effectively, only a tool to aid my investigation, and turning it into something that is now, I hope, readable. That I had only met Susan and her husband Paul Simmonds when they became near neighbours, and friends, shortly before Paul Cooney suggested I should try to find a publisher, is one of life's happier coincidences.

Last, but by no means least, I must thank Maureen MacGlashan, who kindly reviewed an early draft of the text for me. She introduced me to the notion of my 'target audience', which I had not previously considered, and also directed me away from the more controversial and confrontational style that I had adopted. I hope she approves of the finished article that she helped to shape."

Without each of the above this book would not have been finished or published.

Stephen Dudley
Genneteil, France
May 2013

Stained glass from St Mary's Church,
Saxlingham Nethergate, Norfolk

The objective

This book is an account of my investigation into the chronology of the life of the man usually referred to as Jesus Christ or Jesus of Nazareth. I had just one aim for this endeavour: to produce a chronology for his life that is both consistent with the historical record and that accommodates each and every fragment of temporal evidence that resides within the four canonical gospels of the New Testament. I shall begin by giving a brief summary of my conclusions.

The chronology[1]

Event	During the years
The birth of Jesus	10 BCE to 7 BCE
The beginning of Jesus' public life at Bethania	22 CE to 26 CE
The first Passover of Jesus' public life	23 CE to 26 CE
The baptism at Aenon	26 CE to 29 CE
The arrest of John	27 CE to 29 CE
The death of John the Baptist	27 CE to 35 CE
The crucifixion of Jesus	33 CE to 36 CE

I have elected to begin in this way for two reasons. First, although many others have carried out similar investigations over the centuries, I have never encountered one that has succeeded in achieving the aim that I set myself and that I detailed above. Second, the journey we are about to take is not linear: it sets out to be sequential but occasionally wanders up blind alleys, often requires us to make a diversion and frequently doubles back on itself. At the end of each

---

1 Please see pages 17–22 for an explanation of the dating conventions used in this book.

section of this investigation I summarize my results, but these summaries are not themselves conclusions, like milestones written in stone, they are merely status reports, as they are frequently changed by what follows, in a process of gradual refinement. I did not choose this methodology so much as find it imposed on me by the nature of the evidence.

The ranges of years for each of the above events may seem disappointingly broad, but this is for reasons that will become evident as you read on. I have not selected precise dates within any of these ranges, but have presented only the conclusions supported by the evidence. Nevertheless, I believe that what I have arrived at here is the chronological matrix within which the truth resides. It also provides possible alternative explanations for the parts played by events like the massacre of the innocents and the census of Quirinius, which are admittedly conjectural, but which support the chronology without being required by it.

My investigation has nothing to do with faith, or the lack of it and, when I began it, I had no particular chronological destinations in mind, no theories and no preferences. My results are what the evidence requires them to be, and I believe that they are impossible to improve on without resorting to surmise or invention. Unless, that is, there is either a compelling logic or further direct evidence of which I am unaware, which I freely admit is possible.

Stained glass from the church of St Peter Mancroft, Norwich

1

Preparing the way

In order to maintain a consistent approach to this investigation it was first of all necessary to set myself a clear set of guidelines. These guidelines grew with the investigation as I encountered situations for which I had previously made inadequate or no provision. I present these guidelines so that you may both understand the process and use them to assure yourself that I have followed them assiduously.

Of source documents and their authors

There are no truly contemporary documents available to us that chronicle the events of the life of Jesus. If any of his followers, or detractors, kept a journal of events it failed to survive, possibly because of the wholesale destruction of documents that occurred after the fall of Jerusalem (70 CE), although there is a possibility that one or two such documents survived long enough to be referenced by later writers. The nearest sources we have to being contemporary can be found in the New Testament of the Christians' Holy Bible: specifically the four canonical Gospels. All evidence indicates that these Gospels were written and published after Jesus' death but probably before the end of the first century CE.

The works of Josephus are also of great importance in this endeavour. Although they too were written in the latter part of the first century CE they do not specifically address the life of Jesus, but they do provide a fairly comprehensive history of the region which includes the years during which Jesus walked the earth. This enables us to locate certain key events from the Gospels in the historical timeline.

The canonical Gospels

There are, of course, many different variants and translations of the Bible. I am not a scholar of languages, nor do I think it is essential to use a Greek or Hebrew version for my purpose, although I refer sometimes to the research of those who have studied different versions in depth. It became necessary, however, for me to select a single translation, for consistency and so that differences between versions would not create false problems in this work. I chose to work exclusively with the New English Bible (NEB) for two reasons. First, I believe it to be the easiest English version to understand, because of its lack of arcane phrasing and vocabulary, and second, I believe it to be the most accurate version available in the English language. The methodology and scholarship behind the NEB and its successor, the Revised English Bible, is prodigious and impressive, as you will discover if you read its Preface and Introduction.

It would be useful to this investigation if it were possible to know the order in which the four Gospels were written and/or published, as this could help us identify possible sources and influences for each. But unfortunately there is no consensus amongst scholars regarding this. The principal reason for this situation is the very broad range of dates suggested for the Gospel of Matthew, which allows it to be placed almost anywhere in the order. Although there is a high degree of support for recognizing that Mark's Gospel came first and John's last, this is far from universally accepted as fact. Hence, I believe, we cannot rely on order to help with this investigation, and I shall include no explanation, hypothesis or theory that requires it.

Table 1 gives the years associated with the date of writing/ publishing for each of the four canonical Gospels.

Before we turn to authorship of the four Gospels it is necessary to point out some facts about their content. There is almost universal agreement on the following aspects of the four Gospels. The common content, together with the

Table 1

Author	Dates associated
Matthew	36 to 134 CE (with several gaps)
Mark	40 CE, 43 CE, 50 to 67 CE and c. 70 CE
Luke	early 60s CE, later decades of 1st century CE
John	50 to 55 CE, 65 to 85 CE, 90 to 100 CE

similarities of sequence and presentation, in the Gospels of Mark, Matthew and Luke indicate that all three shared a common source. This source is either one of these three Gospels or it is an earlier source, not known of in any more detail, and as far as we know no longer in existence, which is usually referred to as the Q-document. For this reason these Gospels are often referred to as the Synoptic Gospels. Also, to account for the additional information that appears in both Matthew and Luke, two other hypothetical documents are sometimes suggested as the sources: the M-document and the L-document respectively.

The Fourth Gospel, that of John, is devoid of this influence and its content is substantially different. There is a large corpus of unique material together with a smattering of material that narrates events that are contained in the Synoptic Gospels, but in a way that can be quite different.

The only conclusion possible from this is that, at the time of writing, none of the Synoptists had had access to or knowledge of the Fourth Gospel, and that its author had had no knowledge of, or access to, either the Synoptists' source document, or the Synoptic Gospels themselves. Because of this there is a condition that I shall apply when comparing evidence from within the Synoptics with that of the Fourth Gospel: when the accounts in the Synoptics agree with each other and not with the Fourth this will be regarded as a one-all draw and not as a three to one victory to the Synoptists.

We must now consider whether anything more useful to our purpose can be garnered from the Evangelists themselves.

The four Evangelists

It is believed by many that the identities of the four Evangelists are known, although the Gospels themselves were all originally circulated without attribution.

Matthew is believed by many to have been one of the twelve Apostles: Matthew Levi, the ex-collector of taxes. This identification began with the early Christian bishop Papias of Hieropolis (100–140 CE), who first credited a Matthew with authorship, although it was not until towards the end of the second century CE that the association between Papias's Matthew and the apostle Matthew Levi became established. Biblical scholars also believe that the gospel is based on the Q-document and/or the Gospel of Mark and either a hypothetical M-document or the author's own recollections. This seems to beg the question why Matthew needed to base his Gospel on anything other than his own recollections if he was one of the twelve Apostles. I would add to this the opinion that it seems even more unlikely that one of the twelve would know nothing of any of the unique events narrated in the Fourth Gospel.

Since Papias did not specifically name Matthew Levi as the author, there is another obvious candidate: the Matthew usually referred to as Mattathias, the thirteenth Apostle, who replaced Judas Iscariot.

As the knowledge shown by the author of Matthew's Gospel concerning the early part of Jesus' public life is as limited as that of Mark and Luke, I believe it is unsafe to regard him as one of Jesus' earliest followers. It also seems unlikely that someone who was so ignorant of the early history shown in the Fourth Gospel could have been a part of Jesus' entourage much earlier than the appointment of the 70/72 apostles referred to by Luke:

After this the Lord appointed a further seventy-two[12] and
sent them on ahead in pairs to every town and place he
was going to visit himself.

(Luke 10: 1)

Probably the author joined the movement later than this,
maybe even after Jesus' death.

Mark is believed by many to have been John Mark, who some
believe was one of the 70/72 disciple/apostles appointed
by Jesus, and the same John Mark who later became a
companion of Simon Peter on his apostolic mission, which in
its turn leads to the belief that the Gospel was a collection of
Simon Peter's sermons. There seems to be a lot of 'believing'
going on here, but on what is it all based?

The earliest suggestion that John Mark was one of the
70/72 seems to come from a list attributed to Hippolytus of
Rome (c. 170–235 CE) who was a disciple of Irenaeus, who
was a disciple of Polycarp, who was a disciple of John the
Apostle. This must have been drawn up a long time after
the events. But the belief that John Mark, the companion
of Simon Peter, was the author came from none other than
Papias of Hieropolis, who also said that John Mark 'had one
purpose only – to leave out nothing that he had heard, and
to make no misstatement about it'. But where did Hippolytus
and Papias, writing over a hundred years after the events in
question, get this information? No one seems to know. So
once again, I believe we have to treat the authorship of this
gospel in much the same way as that of Matthew.

Luke is believed to have been the same author who compiled
the Acts of the Apostles. This seems a reasonable assumption
as the introduction of both books defers to the patronage of
a Theophilus, the author of the Acts refers to his previous
book, and the style of both is similar. The passage in the

2 Here the NEB footnote says 'some witnesses read seventy'.

Acts (16: 10) where the author switches from third to first person shows us quite clearly when he arrived on the scene: after Paul of Tarsus's conversion and just before his trial in Jerusalem. To assume that he appeared as early as the 70/72 new apostles, as does Hippolytus, seems to me to be without foundation, because surely if he had been one of the 70/72, he would have found a way of telling us so in his Gospel. So we cannot assume any earlier involvement than that shown in the Acts of the Apostles. I have no problem with the author being called Luke, but there is no reference to anyone of that name in the Gospels.

John is believed by many to have been John Boanerges, a Galilean fisherman, brother of James, son of Zebedee and Salome, one of the very first of Jesus' disciples and one of the twelve Apostles. If this is correct then his Gospel should be the most authentic of them all, even if all of the other Evangelists were who 'tradition' requires them to have been. But where does this belief come from? Once again it begins with second-century CE 'tradition', but no source is identifiable, so presumably it has been lost during the intervening years.

I have several problems with this identification:

- According to Mark (5: 37) only John, Peter and James were witnesses to the raising of Jairus's daughter.
- According to Matthew (17: 1) only John, Peter and James were witnesses to Jesus' transfiguration.
- According to Matthew (26: 37) only John, Peter and James were witnesses to his torment of doubt in the garden at Gethsemane.
- According to Luke (22: 8) only John and Peter were sent by Jesus to make preparations for the Last Supper.
- According to the Fourth Gospel (19: 26–27), as Jesus hung on the cross he said to his mother, '"Mother, there is your son"; and, to the disciple (whom he loved), "There is your mother".'

Yet there is no mention in the Fourth Gospel of the first four of these events. Surely if the author of the Fourth Gospel had been John the apostle he would not have failed to mention any of these important events in his own Gospel. Had he done so, he might well have referred to himself as 'the disciple whom Jesus loved' and we would have had real proof that John and this disciple were indeed the same person. But he did not.

The last of these references, from the Fourth Gospel, makes little sense if the beloved disciple had been John. Salome is believed to have been the sister of Jesus' mother, Mary. She was also the wife of Zebedee and the mother of this John, and she was standing next to her sister at the crucifixion! Why would Jesus have 'given' John to his mother while John's own mother was alive and present?

None of this is conclusive, but my objections seem to me to be based on something rather more substantial than the 'tradition' that suggested John as the author in the first place. So if John was not the author of the Fourth Gospel, who was? Another disciple, perhaps?

There are some references in the Fourth Gospel to 'other disciples', one of whom might be the 'beloved disciple'. The first occurs at Bethania immediately after John the Baptist identifies Jesus as 'the Lamb of God' to two of his own disciples (John 1: 36). These disciples followed Jesus, and one of them is then identified as 'Andrew, Simon Peter's brother' (John 1: 42) but the other remains anonymous. This disciple is usually assumed to have been John Boanerges, the son of Zebedee, but there is nothing in the remainder of the text to suggest that either of the Boanerges brothers were even at Bethania.

Then John 21: 1–2 says that shortly after the resurrection Jesus showed himself to some of his disciples by the sea of Tiberias, and lists them as Simon Peter and Thomas the twin, Nathanael of Cana-in-Galilee, the sons of Zebedee (James and John Boanerges) and two other disciples. So clearly neither of these 'two other disciples' was John Boanerges. A little later the author of the Fourth Gospel tells us:

> Peter turned and saw following them the disciple whom Jesus loved, who had lain close to his breast at the supper and had said, 'Lord, who is it that is going to betray you?' When Peter saw him, he said to Jesus, 'Lord, what about this man?' Jesus said to him, 'If it is my will that he remain until I come, what is that to you? Follow me!' The saying spread abroad among the brethren that this disciple was not to die; yet Jesus did not say to him that he was not to die, but, 'If it is my will that he remain until I come, what is that to you?' This is the disciple who is bearing witness to these things, and who has written these things; and we know that his testimony is true.
>
> (John 21: 20–24)

Some researchers argue that from this passage we can only conclude that the 'beloved disciple' was one of the 'two other disciples'. I disagree. From this passage we can only conclude that Simon Peter was not the 'beloved disciple' and hence was not the author of the Fourth Gospel. Here our elusive narrator might well be teasing us by naming himself for the first time in this, the last episode of his Gospel, and he might not have named the two 'other disciples' for any number of reasons. If this were so it would imply that the 'beloved disciple' was one of four men: Thomas, Nathanael, John Boanerges and his brother James. Of these I would favour Nathanael, as none of the Synoptists mention him, but in truth we just cannot know from the information at our disposal.

I remain unconvinced that John Boanerges was the author of the Fourth Gospel. I believe it most probable that the author was not one of the twelve, but was more likely to have been one of the other followers of Jesus who usually worked behind the scenes making preparations and enabling Jesus' mission. Hugh Schonfield, in *The Passover Plot* (1965), also advocated the existence of such a group, and speculated that many of those who were not of the twelve, but who move in and out of the narrative from time to time throughout Jesus' life, belonged to this group. These are people like Nicodemus,

Joseph of Arimathea, Mary Magdalene, Lazarus, Simon the leper, the provider of the ass on Palm Sunday and the owner of the house where the Last Supper was held. It might even be possible that Nathanael falls into this group, as none of the other Evangelists name him as one of the twelve, and there is no list of the twelve in the Fourth Gospel. The author of the Fourth Gospel might also have been one of this group.

From the above I believe we can conclude that:

- None of the Gospels were written by one of the twelve Disciples/Apostles.
- Only the author of the Fourth Gospel was with Jesus from the beginning of his public life, at Bethania, until his execution at Golgotha, though not without interruption.
- Luke is the only Evangelist whom we can reliably identify.
- Luke was the latest of the Evangelists to enter the story himself, being the only one who definitely did not do so until after Jesus' crucifixion. The downside of this is that all of his knowledge of events was second-hand at best. The upside is that he was the only one of the Evangelists who definitely researched his subject.
- The moment at which Matthew and Mark entered the story is indefinite, as are their identities, and their status when they did so is unknown.

It is germane to point out here that I recognize that the Fourth Gospel as we know it today is probably quite different in certain aspects from how it was when first written. One such aspect is the apologetic nature of the references to the Romans in this Gospel (although it is not exactly pro-Roman). Specialists in language have found indications in the original-language version (in Greek) that this is unlikely to have been a feature of the original draft. All of this suggests that there might have been an earlier version which has since disappeared. Perhaps for consistency we should call this the J-document. We can only hope that during the Romanizing process the chronological information in this

Gospel survived unchanged and intact, otherwise this, and every other chronology that has preceded it, would just be a pointless academic exercise.

Before leaving this section it is worth considering some comments in Klaus Berger's book *Kommentar Zum Neuen Testament* (2011). First Berger says:

> Even when there is only a single attestation ... one must suppose, until the contrary is proven, that the Evangelists did not intend to deceive their readers, but rather to inform them concerning historical events ...

 He is correct here; there is no reason to believe that any of the Evangelists intended to convey anything other than a true account. It was what they believed. But Berger goes on to say:

> ... to contest the historicity of this account on mere suspicion exceeds every imaginable competence of historians.

This I take issue with. There are many reasons why an account may contain incorrect historical information other than the honest intentions of the author. It is our duty as investigators to always treat every reference with a degree of scepticism.

All of this is pertinent to this investigation.

The unwritten gospel

There exists another 'gospel' that has no specific name, that does not appear in the Bible and yet with which all Christians are familiar. A version of it first appeared in written form around 150–175 CE, when it was known as the Diatesseron, but it had fallen into disuse by the fifth century CE, by which time it had been more or less universally replaced by the four canonical Gospels of the New Testament. The Diatesseron was constructed by Tatian, an Assyrian and early Christian writer and theologian, who 'harmonized' the four canonical gospels into a single narrative.

Today there is no officially recognized written equivalent of the Diatesseron, although there is a widely accepted but unwritten synthesis of the four Gospels that we all recognize. One accessible example of it is the 1977 Franco Zeffirelli television series entitled *Jesus of Nazareth,* and the book *Man of Nazareth* (1982) based on the series, both of which were written by Anthony Burgess. Because this synthesis is both unwritten and unofficial, it is not definitive and each individual Christian probably perceives it in their own way. The nearest thing to an official version that I have been able to uncover appears in the *New Advent Catholic Encyclopaedia.*

This synthesis is sometimes referred to as the Christian consensus,[3] and its existence is important to this investigation because it is this that is usually the uncredited framework on which other chronologies of Jesus' life have been based. I too shall use it as the basis for my investigation, initially at least.

Exactly how this consensus is constructed will become clearer as this investigation progresses, but a brief (and very simplified) explanation might be useful here. It consists of the insertion of the unique section from the Fourth Gospel, John 1: 35 to 4: 42, between Mark 1: 13 and 1: 14, and other parts from John, Matthew and Luke slipped in wherever seems most appropriate.

Josephus: a brief biography

Josephus Flavius wrote *The Jewish Wars* and *Antiquities of the Jews* around 75 CE and 94 CE respectively. Together they comprise a history of the period immediately prior to, during, and after the events that are the focus of this investigation. Like the Gospels they have been tampered with at various times in

---

3 This term was originally coined by Michael Baigent and Richard Leigh in their 1991 book *The Dead Sea Scrolls Deception.*

their history, but the additions are allegedly usually fairly easy to spot. Josephus's life and circumstances colour his narrative, so it is pertinent here to give a brief synopsis of his life.

Yosef ben Matityahu was born in 37 CE, an ethnic Jew of 'priestly and royal ancestry'. He became a priest in Jerusalem and fought against the Romans in the First Jewish–Roman War of 66–73 CE. In 67 CE he was a rebel commander in Galilee when his forces were besieged at Jupiter by the Roman army, under Vespasian and Titus. After the town had fallen the defenders committed suicide en masse in preference to being captured. Josephus by his own admission survived by deceit, and became a Roman prisoner with the only other survivor. He was released in 69 CE when he defected to the victorious Romans. He played a negotiating role for them in the siege of Jerusalem, and witnessed its destruction after the siege. In 71 CE he went to Rome, having accepted the patronage of the ruling Flavian dynasty, and became a Roman citizen. Later he returned to Israel and was with the Roman troops who entered Masada in 74 CE, after the besieged rebels committed mass suicide. He died in about 100 CE, reviled by the Jews.

Of other sources and circular reasoning

We have already seen that the only sources that were truly contemporary with the life of Jesus are the Q-document and the prototype for the Gospel of John, and if they ever existed they do so no longer. The four Gospels of the New Testament are next in antiquity, and might or might not have been based on these sources, but were almost certainly written by men who were contemporary with the twelve Apostles, if not with Jesus himself. There is also a great deal of material that was written in the second century CE that is both temptingly ancient and authoritative. This is normally referred to as the 'early tradition' and the 'patristic testimonies', and I believe these documents represent the first attempts to flesh out the bones of knowledge concerning the life of Jesus, beyond that residing in the New Testament. This was an entirely natural, understandable and well-intentioned action from those who came after Jesus and his first disciples, as they laboured to establish and disseminate the religion created in his name.

I believe that we need to regard the chronological information conveyed by these sources with a large degree of scepticism. My reason for this distrust is that, when it comes to 'new' chronological information, they do not share either their reasoning or their sources with us. This can lead to a situation where we might unknowingly fall into the trap of circular reasoning when using their information, as others might have done before.

A simple example should clarify what I mean. Let us say that one of the patriarchs indicates the year in which the crucifixion took place. It might then seem reasonable to use that year to help us to find, or corroborate, the year in which Jesus began his ministry. But it is quite possible that the patriarch himself used what he believed was the year of the beginning of the ministry to find the year of Jesus' execution.

As we know from contemporary publications, something that is not true, but that is put down in writing and published, can easily acquire a spurious credibility, especially as it is picked up and repeated by others. This kind of false knowledge pollutes our understanding of actual events, whether they took place yesterday or in the first century CE. So for this reason I shall deliberately avoid using the dates found in these sources for any temporal calculations that I make, although I might use them as reference points.

In contrast, a few unrelated sources are potentially useful because they are quite separate from the Christian consensus, either in its early days or more recently. Most of them are Roman, simply because these are the best preserved of the sources of that era. They include lists of consuls, histories, and writing on gravestones and monuments. All of these are secular rather than religious in nature, and because the historical personages who are mentioned in them are sometimes also mentioned in the Gospels, they can assist us in placing the events of Jesus' life in the historical timeline. There is no need to introduce these miscellaneous sources at this point: they are attributed and referenced (in the text or the notes) when they are employed.

Of secondary sources

Occasionally in this investigation I shall make reference to information cited by other researchers, for which I have been unable to access the original source. This is not a safe practice, as the information has already been interpreted by the author of the secondary source. However, I shall do this only when the information provided is too significant to ignore, and I shall always indicate when I am using such a reference. How this information is then used in this chronology depends on a number of factors that vary from case to case, so I shall make them clear each time this occurs.

Modus operandi

There are two remaining tasks before we can begin this investigation, both of which are crucial to this undertaking. The first concerns the very framework of chronology: time, or rather the measurement of time, the way in which we describe its passage, and how the way in which this has been done over the last two thousand years has adversely affected our ability to be accurate and certain of dates. The second is the requirement to have a transparent and consistent methodology for using the available evidence. If we fail to address either of these tasks we would have no firm basis for deduction, and would therefore be left with nothing more than assumption and surmise.

The trouble with time

The Julian calendar was the one in use at the time of the events that are the subject of this investigation. Year one of this calendar, 1 AUC (short for *ab urbe condita*, meaning 'from the founding of the city' of Rome) is taken to have been the year 753 BCE of the Gregorian calendar, the one in use today. This then leads to the following: 753 AUC = 1 BCE and 754 AUC = 1 CE. This is how and why it happened.

The Julian calendar was introduced in the year 709 AUC, which is 45 BCE (Gregorian), and replaced the calendar used previously because it had been inaccurate and required frequent intercalations in order to keep the dates of the equinoxes reasonably constant. Then, in the year 1278 AUC (525 CE in the Gregorian calendar) Dionysius Exiguus[4] advocated that the Julian calendar be restarted from the year that he believed was that of Jesus' birth, making the year 754 AUC the year 1 AD (*anno domini*, 'the year of our lord'). The universal adoption of the Dionysian revision was not immediate, however, but by the time that the Gregorian calendar was introduced, in the year 1582 AD, it had become so. This means that the year 1582 was both the last year of the Dionysian reform of the Julian calendar and the first year of the Gregorian calendar, which also means that the numbering of the years given by the Dionysian revised Julian calendar, both BC and AD, are, to all intents and purposes of this investigation, the same as those given by the BCE and CE years of today's calendar. This would have been easier to follow if, when the Gregorian calendar was initiated, its terminology had also been changed from BC/AD to something else, like BCE/CE for instance, but it was not.

---

4 Dionysius Exiguus (*c* 470–*c* 544 CE) was a Scythian monk who moved to Rome in c 500 CE, where he earned a solid reputation as a most learned abbot and was accorded the honorific *abbas* by the Venerable Bede.

Consequently when, during the course of this investigation, I refer to the Julian calendar, it will imply the AUC version and not the Dionysian one. Also I shall use the modern terms BCE and CE to imply the use of the Gregorian calendar and/or the Dionysian AD revision of the Julian calendar, as if they are the same thing, even though this is not strictly correct.

The source documents provide chronological evidence in a variety of different ways. Some of these references can be resolved to a single year and some cannot. By far the most useful are the first group, but they are few and far between. Evidence from the second group is more frequent and more troublesome.

In the twenty-first century by far the most common way of providing a temporal reference is by giving a precise date: a single year (or a specific day in that year). But in the first centuries BCE and CE this was not the case: there is not a single chronological reference in any of the source documents to a calendar year for the occurrence of any event. So why wasn't the perfectly adequate Julian calendar used by the Roman historians and the Christian evangelists? The answer is not clear, but more importantly, we need to consider what was used instead. Roman historians used the Consular List to provide a single unambiguous year, as did Josephus and some of the second-century CE patriarchs of the nascent Christian church.

Here is a reasonably typical example of how the Consular List was used. Halley's comet made one of its periodic appearances in the year that Publius Sulpicius Quirinius was consul. The Consular Lists show that Quirinius held this office, together with Valerius Barbatus, in the year 742 AUC (Julian calendar), which is the year 12 BCE of the Gregorian calendar, so we know that this is the year when the comet was seen.

There is another important aspect of the consular year related to its reliability in providing a single year for an event. Unlike some aspects of Roman life, in which the year began on 1 March and ended on the last day of February, these appointments ran from 1 January until 31 December, so they can be aligned exactly with the Gregorian year. This does not mean that the use of the Consular List guarantees complete accuracy, however. There are ambiguities in the versions of the list that have survived to this day. It seems that sometimes more than the usual two consuls were appointed in a particular year, and one of these extra consuls was also in office in another year. It is also possible that historians or researchers made mistakes, calculating the year of a particular event inaccurately and then assigning the consular reference to an incorrect year. But by and large we should be able to use the consular year associated with a particular event with a degree of confidence.

The Evangelists themselves provided us with no chronological evidence that can be reduced to a single year. This is a great pity, as if they had, there would be no ambiguities and no need for research such as that summarized in this book.

Another possible way of identifying the specific year for an event is for it to be correlated with a historical event that is independently dateable. For example, Luke (2: 1–2) tells us that Jesus was born in the year of the census of Quirinius. Unfortunately it is not possible to date the census with pinpoint accuracy: it is generally reckoned to have occurred in either or both of 6 and 7 CE. However, there are not many references in the Bible to occurrences in the same year as historical events significant enough to be remembered and located in the historical timeline. Much more frequently the reference is to a well-known event such as the death of an emperor, and gives a period of elapsed time between it and the other biblical event. Although it might seem otherwise, evidence presented in this way is not as accurate as that derived from a consular reference, as I shall now do my best to explain by using an event that is of no historical significance, but for which the date is known exactly.

I was born on 10 June 1948. This means I was 'one year old' on 10 June 1949, or more correctly, 10 June 1949 was the first anniversary of my birth. According to the conventions we use today for giving people's ages, I remained a 'one-year-old' until midnight on 9 June 1950. Thus there are two actual years for which it is correct to say that I was 'one year old': 1949 and 1950. Furthermore, as I was actually born in 1948, it is also true to say that 1948 was the 'actual first year' of my life. But it is also true to say that the 12-month period from 10 June 1948 to 9 June 1949 was the first elapsed year of my life, which makes 10 June 1949 the first day of the second elapsed year of my life as well as the first anniversary of my birth. If we now apply this information to my being 30, we find that the year 1977 was the actual 30th year of my life, that the '30th elapsed year' of my life began on 10 June 1977 and ended on 9 June 1978, that 10 June 1978 was the 30th anniversary of my birth, and that I was '30 years of age' until 9 June 1979.

Thus there are three calendar years that can be associated with being in one's 30th year and with having, or being, the age of 30, as there is with each and every age. This can be presented more succinctly as 'the anniversary year +/- 1 year'. We must keep these three years in mind whenever we attempt to use a chronological reference from the source documents that describes a period of elapsed time from a dateable historical event. It is not always necessary to assign all three of these years to each piece of evidence, but it is almost always necessary to apply two, and this is always dependent on the exact context and nature of the evidence.

Another factor also has a bearing on how we use this kind of temporal information. It is highly likely that some societies used only ordinal years when talking of elapsed time. In other words the attainment of someone's 13th year may well have been the more usual way of signifying an age than being 12 years old.[5] We can by no means be certain that the judaic population of Israel was not such a society, at the time with

---

5   In the epilogue of his book *Jesus of Nazareth: The infancy years* (2012), Joseph Ratzinger clearly demonstrates his misunderstanding of this fact.

which this investigation is concerned.

We shall encounter another category of chronological evidence that makes use of elapsed time and produces a range of possible years. From these references all we can hope to achieve is an earliest possible year and a latest possible year. The first and most common of these references are in the general form 'in the reign of ...', 'during the governorship of ...' and 'when ... was high priest'. But often it is not possible to assign an exact year to either the beginning and/or the end of these ranges, in which case we have to use the earliest earliest possible year and the latest latest possible year allowed by our research, which often and unsurprisingly leads to a disappointingly large range of possible years.

Another subset of evidence in this category is one used occasionally by Josephus: the Olympiads. These are sequential four-year periods, the first of which began on 1 July 776 BCE and ended on 30 June 772 BCE. Use of the Olympiads for dating other events was less popular than using the Consular List, possibly because these four-year periods ran from mid-year to mid-year through five actual years, making the related dates awkward to calculate.

In this investigation we shall need to know the years of the 184th and 185th Olympiads. The easiest way of finding the first year of any Olympiad is by applying this formula: the first year of the nth Olympiad = $776 - 4(n - 1)$. (This can be checked by applying it to the first two Olympiads:

The first year of the 1st Olympiad	$= 776 - 4(1 - 1)$
	$= 776 - 0 = 776$ BCE
The first year of the 2nd Olympiad	$= 776 - 4(2 - 1)$
	$= 776 - (4 \times 1) = 772$ BCE
Therefore the first year of the	
184th Olympiad	$= 776 - 4(184 - 1)$ BCE
	$= 776 - (4 \times 183)$ BCE
	$= 776 - 732$ BCE
	$= 44$ BCE

Similarly the 185th Olympiad began on 1 July 40 BCE. We shall put this information to good use in the Nativity section of the investigation.

We have now examined an example of each type of temporal evidence that the source documents have provided for us, but we have not yet finished with considerations of time. There remains one particularly irritating problem that requires explanation. It concerns the ways in which the years themselves have been numbered.

We have already seen that 753 AUC = 1 BCE and 754 AUC = 1 CE. To calculate a period of elapsed time we must subtract the number value of the earlier year from that of the later year. Doing so for the Julian calendar gives us $754 - 753 = 1$. Doing the same for the Gregorian gives us $1 - 1 = 0$. These two results contradict each other. The years BCE should properly be negative numbers but if we do the calculation again we find that $1 - (-1) = 1 + 1 = 2$.

So whichever way we use the Gregorian years here, we get a different result from that given by the Julian calendar. This means that each and every time we try to make a calculation of elapsed time that crosses the BCE/CE frontier we arrive at an answer that is different from that arrived at by using the Julian calendar.

Common sense tells us that the answer given by the Julian calendar must be correct, because it gives us the answer we expect. This does not mean that the answers given by the Gregorian calendar are incorrect. They are not, but the reasons for this are complex and, I believe, need not be considered in detail here. It is enough for us to know that the problem exists, and that it is necessary to find a consistent and simple way of avoiding it in order to ensure that we do not introduce errors into our calculations of elapsed time.

For me the obvious and easiest way is to make all calculations using the Julian calendar. However the easiest way to present them to readers is, I believe, using the Gregorian calendar, so this is what I use in the body of the text here. (Table 4, pp. 117 ff, shows the comparative dates in the different formats.)

The rules of engagement

When I first began this work it was not an investigation as such. It was just something I did when I had some spare time. It was only when I began to make time for it that it became serious, and an investigation, and that I found the need to keep track of what I was finding in a more organized way. Inevitably, or so it seems now, I discovered the need to define parameters for myself that allowed the data itself to lead me, rather than the opposite. Only then did I begin to make real progress. These parameters became my rules of engagement, and they ensured that the investigation remained objective and consistent. These rules are:

1. Every piece of direct historical association in the Gospels and the Acts must have a place in the narrative. Nothing can be ignored or excluded unless and until inclusion becomes totally untenable. These associations must take precedence over all other content.
2. Non-numerical references to elapsed time in the Gospels and Acts must be treated with a large degree of caution. There is ample circumstantial internal evidence that phrases like 'the next day' might not mean exactly that. Words like 'later' and 'after' can well indicate a lack of knowledge of the actual elapsed time between the two events that they link, and therefore must only be taken to mean that the second event followed the first. Also there are occasional abrupt changes from one episode to another, and from one location to another, that give no indication of elapsed time and should not be assumed, therefore, to mean continuity.
3. The counting of recurrent annual events, such as Passovers, should be regarded as a minimum, not an absolute value. The assumption that *all* occurrences of these events are recorded in the Gospels is unsafe, so those mentioned will remain a minimum unless other evidence is available or a compelling logic suggests that all occurrences *have* been recorded.

4. The order of events in the Gospels is not definitive. This is easily shown by listing events from each of the Gospels side by side, but it will become evident during the course of this investigation. We may assume, however, that where linking words like 'later' and 'after' have been used, order is implied or intended unless or until we discover other evidence to the contrary.

5. Events that are mentioned in the New Testament only once and for which there is no corroborative evidence elsewhere should be treated with caution. But lack of corroboration is not proof that the event did not occur.

6. Where a range of dates is possible for an event I shall not eliminate or select dates from the range available *unless* other evidence is available or a compelling logic suggests itself that reduces, eliminates or otherwise selects on our behalf.

I have used the word 'logic' here as this must go hand-in-glove with deduction for an enterprise of this nature. It is by the application of these instruments, rather than faith, that we will bridge the gap between belief and knowledge. We must also be aware of two logical fallacies in this pursuit: *post hoc ergo propter hoc* (after this, therefore because of this) and *cum hoc ergo propter hoc* (with this, therefore because of this). Both concern the assumption of causality without it being proven. The relationship between cause and effect has to be demonstrated, and cannot be claimed simply because of juxtaposition alone.

Stained glass from Trinity
Church, Vendome, France

2

The investigation

There are four events in the life of Jesus for which dates can be derived with any degree of confidence. They are his birth, the beginning of his public life, the beginning of his ministry and his execution. I shall address each of these events in this order, and together they will provide the skeleton for the flesh of this investigation.

Stained glass from the church of Notre Dame, Richelieu, France

Stained glass from the Church of St Mary the Virgin, Banham, Norfolk

The nativity

Dionysius Exiguus must have believed that he knew when Jesus was born when, in the year 535 CE, he proposed to restart the Julian calendar from this event, numbering the year 754 AUC as year 1 AD (*anno domini*) and numbering all the years thereafter accordingly. It is now commonly accepted that he selected the wrong year for Jesus' birth when he made this proposal, which presumes that he calculated the year incorrectly. But as this is one of the significant dates in Jesus' life that this investigation seeks to ascertain, we must suspend judgement until we have completed our own calculations.

The consensus – Part 1

Only two of the four Gospels contain an account of Jesus' birth, Matthew and Luke, and the consensus accommodates each and every element of both accounts. It is the familiar story that Christians celebrate at Christmas, and looks something like this:

- In the time of Herod the Great ... (Matthew 2: 1, Luke 1: 5).
- The priest Zechariah is visited by the angel Gabriel, who tells him that he and his wife Elizabeth will have a son, whose name will be John. Zechariah is struck dumb when he protests that they are too old and his wife is barren (Luke 1: 5–25).
- In the sixth month of Elizabeth's pregnancy Gabriel visits Elizabeth's cousin Mary, who is betrothed to Joseph, at Nazareth, and tells her she too will bear a son whose name is to be Jesus and that he will be 'king over Israel'. She protests her virginity and is told that 'the Holy Spirit will come upon you' and 'the holy child to be born will be called "Son of God"' (Luke 1: 26–38).
- When Joseph hears this news he 'desired to have the

marriage contract set aside' but an angel dissuades him. He takes Mary home to be his wife and has no intercourse with her until after Jesus is born (Matthew 1: 18–25).

- 'About this time' Elizabeth is visited by Mary, who stays with her cousin for about three months. Then, after John is born, Zechariah's voice returns so that he can pronounce his son's name as John, after which he is filled with the Holy Spirit (Luke 1: 39–79).

- Joseph and Mary travel from Nazareth to Bethlehem in order to comply with the requirements of the census. Unable to find proper accommodation, they have to stay in a stable, where Jesus is born (Luke 2: 1–20). By the time of the birth a new star has appeared in the sky to signify the birth of the king of the Jews (Matthew 2: 1–2).

- After the birth of Jesus three shepherds are visited by an angel who tells them of the birth of the Messiah. They go to Bethlehem to find Joseph, Mary and the baby and tell them what the angel has said (Luke 2: 8–20).

- Three magi from the east follow the star to Jerusalem, where they ask Herod where the king of the Jews was born. Herod's astrologers send them to Bethlehem after they have promised to return and tell him where the child can be found (Matthew 2: 1–8).

- The magi arrive in Bethlehem, at which time the star stops. They present gifts and praise the new arrival. Then, after being warned in a dream, they decide not to honour their promise to Herod, and return to their home by a different route (Matthew 2: 9–12).

- After they have left, an angel appears to Joseph in a dream and tells him that Herod plans to find Jesus and kill him. He then advises the family to escape to Egypt (Matthew 13 to 15).

- Joseph and Mary 'present' Jesus at the Temple in Jerusalem (Luke 2: 21–28).

- When the magi fail to return to Jerusalem Herod orders all children of Bethlehem under the age of three to be killed (Matthew 2: 16–18).

- After being warned of this by an angel, Joseph takes his family to Egypt (Matthew 2: 14–15).

- After Herod's death Joseph takes Mary and Jesus from Egypt to Nazareth as Herod's successor, Archelaus, has become king and they are afraid to go to Judaea (Matthew 2: 19–21; Luke 2: 39–40).

You will find, on close examination, that some of these references sit uneasily in their consensus place. None more so than the last, as Matthew says that the family *settled* in Nazareth after Herod's death as they were afraid to *return* to Bethlehem, because of Archelaus's accession, whereas Luke says that, after they had presented Jesus at the Temple, they *returned* to Galilee and their own town of Nazareth.

We shall now begin the search for the year of Jesus' birth by looking at the one piece of evidence on which Matthew and Luke appear to agree: that Jesus was born during the reign of Herod the Great.

Of two Herods

Matthew tells us quite simply that 'Jesus was born at Bethlehem in Judaea during the reign of Herod' (2: 1) while Luke begins by saying 'In the days of Herod king of Judaea' (1: 5) before going on to describe the circumstances of Jesus' birth at Bethlehem. Neither of these two Evangelists tells us to which Herod they were referring. Why then is it almost universally accepted that the nativity of Jesus occurred during the reign of Herod the Great? Could it be because there was only one king of Judaea named Herod? It could not, because there were two: Herod the Great and Herod Archelaus. There were also two other kings who either took the name Herod themselves or to whom posterity has gifted it: Herod Antipas and Herod Philip. From this we have to accept that it is by no means self-evident that either Matthew or Luke were referring to the reign of Herod the Great. So first we must look into the two Nativity Gospels more closely to see if there is any contextual evidence to help us with this matter.

Technically, of course, none of the sons of Herod the

Great were entitled to be called 'king', but this did not stop either Josephus or the Evangelists from doing so. Unusually, perhaps, it is what they have written that is important here, and not the absolute truth.

Matthew follows his announcement that Jesus was born during the reign of Herod with a description of the visit of the Magi, the flight to Egypt and the 'massacre of the innocents' (2: 2–18), before telling us that Herod had died (2: 19). The account goes on to describe how Joseph received the news from an angel that it was safe to return to Israel, but decided to go to Galilee rather than Judaea (2: 20–21) after hearing that Archelaus had succeeded his father as king of Judaea (2: 22). It is easily established that Herod the Great was the father of Archelaus and that the son became king of Judaea on the death of the father. Therefore the context here confirms that the Herod of Matthew's version of the nativity can only have been Herod the Great.

Luke, on the other hand, places the following events during the reign of *his* Herod: the circumstances leading to the miraculous conceptions of John the Baptist and Jesus, the birth of John (1: 5–80), and the circumstances of Jesus' own birth, during the census of Quirinius (2: 1–7). It is this census that provides us with the contextual corroboration that the Herod of Luke's Gospel must have been Herod Archelaus, and not Herod the Great. This is because of the apparent similarities between the census described by Luke (2: 1–2) and the census taken by Quirinius on the deposition of Herod Archelaus, and recorded by Josephus (*Antiquities of the Jews (AJ)*, book XVIII, ch. 1, p. 1).

This on its own is not conclusive of anything, however. Luke is believed to have been a Greek and a gentile before his conversion, and although we know from the Acts of the Apostles that he visited Jerusalem with Paul of Tarsus, it does not necessarily follow that he was conversant with either the political geography or the history of the region fifty years or more before the time when he wrote his gospel. Before Josephus it is unlikely that there would have been many, if any, sources for him to study on the subject, and we can in no way be certain that he had access to either of Josephus's books. All we do know about his sources is what he told Theophilus in the introduction to his Gospel:

> Many writers have undertaken to draw up an account of the events that have happened among us, following the traditions handed down to us by the original eyewitnesses and servants of the Gospel.
>
> (Luke 1: 1–2)

As his knowledge was second-hand, at best, we have to allow for the possibility that Luke might not even have known to which Herod the story he was recounting referred. But, so far as the evidence that he has passed on is concerned, it suggests that Jesus was born during the reign of Herod Archelaus and not during the reign of his father, Herod the Great, as Matthew's evidence requires.

So for the purposes of this investigation, we have no alternative other than to consider both possibilities.

The reign of Herod the Great

His accessions

There are two dates of accession associated with Herod the Great becoming king of the Jews. The first occurred on his election to this position by the Roman Senate, and the second on the liberation of Jerusalem from, and execution of, the previous incumbent, Antigonus. These two beginnings to his reign are generally referred to as his accessions *de jure* and *de facto* respectively. To take the beginning of Herod's reign *de jure* first, we find that Josephus relates the following:

> Antony informed them further, that it was for their advantage in the Parthian war that Herod should be king. This seemed good to all the senators; and so they made a decree accordingly .... And thus did this man

[Herod] receive the kingdom, having obtained it on the hundred and eighty-fourth olympiad, when Caius Domitius Calvinus was consul the second time, and Caius Asinius Pollio [the first time].

(Josephus, *AJ* book XIV, ch. xiv, paras 4 and 5)

The 184th Olympiad began on 1 July 44 BCE and lasted until 30 June 40 BCE, and the Consular List indicates that the year of the consulship of Calvinus and Pollio was 40 BCE. Combining these two pieces of information suggests that Herod's election by the Senate could only have occurred during the first half of the year 40 BCE. Unfortunately however Appian,[6] in his *Historia Romana*, places this event in the year 39 BCE. The Appian reference comes from several secondary sources, none of which identify or give the relevant passage. Consequently, as it leads us to a single year, I am forced to assume it came from a consular reference, to either Marcius Censorinus or Calvisius Sabinus, and treat it with equal value to the consular reference given by Josephus.

Since these two authorities do not agree, we must allow for the two possible years of **40 BCE and 39 BCE** for the beginning of Herod's reign *de jure*.

Turning now to Herod's accession *de facto,* Josephus says:

When the rigor of winter was over, Herod removed his army, and came near to Jerusalem, and pitched his camp hard by the city. Now this was the third year since he had been made king at Rome.

(Josephus, *AJ* book XIV, ch. xv, para. 4)

---

6 Appianus (*c.* 95–165), of Alexandria, was a Roman historian (of Greek ethnicity) who flourished during the reigns of Trajan, Hadrian and Antoninus Pius. He is commonly known by the anglicized form of his name, Appian. His principal surviving work, known in Latin as *Historia Romana,* was written in Greek in 24 books, before 165 CE, and survives in complete books and considerable fragments (source: Wikipedia).

This destruction befell the city of Jerusalem when Marcus Agrippa and Caninius Gallus were consuls of Rome on the hundred eighty and fifth olympiad, on the third month, on the solemnity of the fast, as if a periodical revolution of calamities had returned since that which befell the Jews under Pompey; for the Jews were taken by him on the same day, and this was after twenty-seven years' time.

(Josephus, *AJ* book XIV, ch. xvi, para. 4)

'The third year since he [Herod] had been made king at Rome' cannot be resolved to a single year. This is because the third year since 40 BCE would have begun in 38 BCE and ended in 37 BCE, while similarly, the third year since 39 BCE is 37 BCE or 36 BCE. So the evidence considered from this reference to elapsed time allows for the range of years from **38 BCE to 36 BCE.**

From the Consular List we find that 37 BCE was the year in which Marcus Vespanius Agrippa and Caninius Gallus were consuls, which year falls nicely within the 185th Olympiad. However, Josephus requires Jerusalem to have fallen in the third month of this Olympiad, which was September of 40 BCE, which cannot be correct if Josephus's information for Herod's accession *de jure* is correct (see Table 2, page 35).

It is believed that Pompey took the city of Jerusalem at the time of the Passover in 63 BCE, and exactly 27 years later is the year 36 BCE, although the actual twenty-seventh year began in 37 BCE. As the first part of 36 BCE falls outside the consulship of Agrippa and Gallus, this strongly suggests that the second fall of Jerusalem occurred at Passover in 37 BCE.

Unfortunately Cassius Dio[7] reported in *his Historia Romana*

---

7   Lucius Cassius Dio Cocceianus (c. 155 or 163/164 CE to after 229 CE), known in English as Cassius Dio, Dio Cassius, or Dio, was a Roman consul and a noted historian writing in Greek. He published a history of Rome in 80 volumes, beginning with the legendary arrival of Aeneas in Italy and continuing up to

that 'the Romans accomplished nothing worthy of note in the region during this year'. Again this comes from secondary sources, without context, so we do not know if Dio said exactly these words, which seems unlikely, or if the lack of notable events was assumed by these secondary sources, from a lack of information in the overall text. Either way we cannot just ignore the information.

It is also pertinent here to point out that I believe one of the pieces of evidence that we have used to find Herod's accession *de facto* is tainted, and that is the year of Pompey's sacking of Jerusalem. My reason for this is that every source I have checked to find the year for this event has given the same answer, 63 BCE, without giving any provenance. There is only one way I know of for deriving that year, and that is by applying the 27 years of elapsed time, suggested by Josephus, to the year 36 CE: the year of the consulship of Agrippa and Gallus. By doing this we arrive at the year (718 AUC − 27 = 691 AUC) 63 BCE for Pompey's victory. This calculation assumes that this is the year of Herod's accession *de facto*, which, if this is so, would make our use of the same information, but in the opposite direction, a bad case of circular reasoning.

It is particularly frustrating for what looked to have been a pretty reliable, and rare, single year for this event to have been eliminated in this way, particularly when Dio has no alternative to offer. This forces us to accept the broadest range we have calculated for Herod's accession *de facto*, which was derived from Herod's accession *de jure*, and leads to the three-year period of elapsed time: **38 to 36 BCE.**

Table 2 shows all of the information we have found that is relevant to the years of Herod's accessions *de jure* and *de facto*. From this we can clearly see that the association of 'the third month of the 185th Olympiad' with Herod's accession *de facto* cannot be correct. We can also see that if this were applied

229 CE, a period of about 1,400 years. He wrote 80 books over 22 years, and many have survived intact or as fragments, providing modern scholars with a detailed perspective on Roman history (source: Wikipedia).

Table 2

Olympiad	Year	Event/source	Event
184th	41 BCE		
	40 BCE	Consulship of Calvinus and Pollio	Herod's accession *de jure* according to Josephus
185th			
	39 BCE	*Historia Romana* (Appian)	Herod's accession *de jure* according to Appian
	38 BCE		
	37 BCE	Consulship of Agrippa and Gallus; according to Cassius Dio nothing of any consequence occurred in Judaea in this year	Possible 27 years after Pompey sacked Jerusalem
	36 BCE		Possible 27 years after Pompey sacked Jerusalem
186th			
	35 BCE		

to the 186th Olympiad it would fall within the range of years we have calculated for the second accession from those of the first. This is not unlikely as it is quite possible here that Josephus simply assumed that, as Herod's first accession occurred during the 184th Olympiad, his second would have

occurred in the *next* Olympiad, the 185th, which we can now
see is not necessarily the case.

There is another point to be considered here, however,
as Josephus states that Jerusalem was sacked 'on the 185th
Olympiad, on the third month, on the solemnity of the
fast'. His claiming that this occurred on the exact 27th
anniversary of Pompey's sacking implies that it was during
the Passover, as the first sacking was believed to have been.
But there is a contradiction here, as Passover occurs in
March, the third month of the Julian year, and Josephus
also claims the second sacking was in the third month of
an Olympiad, which would have been September. Quite
clearly it is impossible for all of these conditions to be
accommodated, and we can only guess at which of them
are correct and which are not. However tempting it may
seem to assume that 37 BCE is the most likely year, as it
accommodates most of the criteria, we cannot simply dismiss
Cassius Dio's indication to the contrary. This leaves us with
no other option than to assign the range of years derived
by adding three years to the year range of his accession *de
jure*.

In summary it is only safe to say that we are left with the
two years of **40 and 39 BCE** for Herod's accession *de jure*, and
one of the three years from **38 to 36 BCE** for his accession *de
facto*. However, it should be noted that, with respect to future
calculations, it is necessary, wherever possible to use the
range given by Herod's accession *de jure* as the starting point,
as the date of his accession *de facto* has been derived directly
from it.

We can now turn our attention to consideration of the
year for:

The death of Herod the Great

Josephus tells us:

> When he [Herod] had done these things, he died …
> having reigned, since he had procured Antigonus to be

slain, thirty-four years; but since he had been declared king by the Romans, thirty-seven.

(Josephus, *AJ* book XVII, ch. viii, para. 1)

If exactly thirty-seven years had elapsed between Herod's accession *de jure* and his death, then his death would have occurred in the range ([714 AUC + 37 =] 751 AUC to [715 AUC + 37 =] 752 AUC) 3 to 2 BCE. But if Josephus was counting actual years we find that the actual 37th year of his reign *de jure* is 4 BCE, if it began in 40 BCE, or 3 BCE if it began in the later year, giving us the total range of 4 to 2 BCE for the possible years of Herod's death.

There is however the additional information, also supplied by Josephus, that a lunar eclipse preceded Herod's death.[8] In context, the reference, although a little vague, seems to place this eclipse just before the Passover of the year in which Herod died. Modern astronomers have calculated that a partial eclipse was visible in this region on 13 March 4 BCE, about twenty-nine days before Passover, and this eclipse is usually taken to be the one referred to by Josephus. There were, however, three other lunar eclipses visible in Judaea around this time, all of them total, and some scholars[9] have argued for each of these. Two occurred in 5 BCE, and the other in 1 BCE.

There may well be proponents for the eclipses of 5 BCE and 1 BCE, but in my view they have no case without other evidence, as both of these years fall outside the range produced by the evidence we have derived from Josephus. The fact that these

---

8   *AJ*, book XVII, ch. vi, para. 4, 'This Matthias the high priest, on the night before that day when the fast was to be celebrated .... But Herod deprived this Matthias of the high priesthoods .... And that very night there was an eclipse of the moon.'

9   Throughout this document I shall use phrases like *some scholars* and *other researchers* where the originator of a particular idea is unknown to me. This is usually because I have encountered the idea in a refutation of it by another scholar or researcher who has not assigned provenance.

eclipses were *total,* while the one of 4 BCE was only *partial,* adds no weight to their argument. That is unless they are advocating that these events are actually causally linked and not just a useful, but completely random, coincidence. It is my opinion that Josephus is more likely to have mentioned the fact that the eclipse was total, if that had been the case, and that it is most likely that the lunar eclipse of 4 BCE is the one that is associated with Herod's death.

Some scholars have found further confirmation for this date in the events that immediately followed Herod's death: the division of his kingdom between three of his sons. The greater part, consisting of Judaea, Idumea and Samaria, was given to Archelaus together with the title of ethnarc, whilst Antipas became tetrarch[10] of Galilee and Peraea, and Philip became tetrarch of the territories east of the Jordan. Once again it is Josephus who provides us with the opportunity to explore the evidence for this.

The references that relate to Antipas seem to contribute nothing towards establishing a year for either his own accession or the death of Herod. For any reader who wishes to confirm this, the relevant references are in the notes.[11]

The two references to Archelaus's reign that Josephus provides only tell us the duration of his reign. It is also unfortunate that these two references seem to contradict each other, but we can still apply this information to calculate a range of years for his deposition, once we have confirmed the year of Herod's death. But we cannot use this *to verify* the year of Herod's death.

---

10 Tetrarchy was the name given by the Romans to a quarter of a province or vassal kingdom, and the title of tetrarch to its ruler. Because Archelaus had been given control over almost half of his father's kingdom Augustus gave him the title ethnarc, being ruler of an 'ethnic group' but of less importance than a king (various sources).

11 *JW,* book II, ch, ix, para. 6; *AJ,* book XVII, ch. vii, paras 1&2, book XVIII, ch. vi, para. 11, and book XIX, ch. viii, para. 2.

Fortunately, when it comes to Philip, Josephus gives us something concrete with which to work:

> About this time it was that Philip, Herod's brother, departed this life, in the twentieth year of the reign of Tiberius, after he had been tetrarch of Trachonitis and Gaulanitis, and of the nation of the Bataneans also, thirty-seven years.
>
> (Josephus, *AJ* book XVIII, ch. iv, para. 6)

(The Herod referred to here is Antipas, as the context clearly indicates.) This provides both the duration of Philip's reign and information about the year of his death, albeit it is not absolute, but relative to the reign of the Emperor Tiberius. There are four significant events and five different years relating to Tiberius's succession to his stepfather Augustus:

4 CE	when Augustus made Tiberius his successor in his will
11 or 12 CE	when Tiberius received his provincial powers
13 CE	when Augustus made Tiberius co-emperor
14 CE	when Augustus died leaving Tiberius as absolute emperor.

I contend that only the last two of these events have any credible claim to represent the year of Tiberius's accession. Therefore the three years that could have been considered as the twentieth year of Tiberius's reign, and hence the year of Philip's death, are from 32 to 34 CE.

If we now combine this range of years with the information that Philip also reigned for 37 years, the accession to his tetrarchy, and hence the death of Herod, occurred in the period from ([785 AUC − 37 =] 748 AUC to [787 AUC − 37 =] 750 AUC) 5 to 3 BCE. This nicely brackets the year we have already derived for the death of Herod, and hence provides further verification that 4 BCE is probably the correct date.

We have not used this new information to calculate the year of Herod's death, only to verify it; so we can also justifiably use it in another way, and take advantage of the rare opportunity provided by having a single year for an event. Adding the length of Philip's reign to the single year we have for Herod's death we arrive at the date of Philip's death: 33 or 34 CE. Now we can compare this range with that we derived for the twentieth year of Tiberius's reign, 32 to 34 CE.

This shows that:

- only the two years of 33 and 34 CE are allowable for the death of Philip
- the death of Herod must have occurred in the year 4 BCE.

From this we can state with some confidence that Herod the Great's reign *de jure* ranged from **40 or 39 BCE to 4 BCE.**

The short reign of Herod Archelaus

We have already ascertained that Archelaus's reign as king of Judaea began when his father died, in 4 BCE. If we now return our attention to Josephus's information regarding the length of Archelaus's reign, we can apply it to the year we have derived for Herod's death with some confidence.

> But in the tenth year of Archelaus's government ... Caesar, upon hearing what certain accusers of his had to say, and what reply he could make, both banished him, and appointed Vienna, a city of Gaul, to be the place of his habitation, and took his money away from him.
>
> (Josephus, *AJ* book XVII, ch. xiii, para. 2)

and:

> in the ninth year of his government he [Archelaus] was banished to Vienna, a city of Gaul, and his effects were put into Caesar's treasury.
>
> (Josephus, *JW* book II, ch. vii, para. 3)

The ninth year of his reign would have begun in 5 CE and ended in 6 CE, when his tenth year began, leaving 7 CE as the year in which the tenth year ended. This seems to give a three-year range of possible years for the deposition of Archelaus. However, the middle of these three years, **6 CE**, seems the most likely for his deposition, as it encompasses part of both the ninth and the tenth elapsed years of Archelaus's reign: the later months of the former and the early months of the latter, which would then account for the two 'different' years given by Josephus.

The reign of Archelaus can now be given, with some confidence, as the range of years from **4 BCE to 6 CE.**

Summary

As Archelaus succeeded his father as king of Judaea it was inevitable that their reigns would prove to be mutually exclusive, but it was still necessary to define both of their reigns as accurately as possible, as this information is central to much of what is to follow. But we are still none the wiser regarding which of these two reigns Luke was referring to, even though the census to which he also refers seems to be the one that characterized the end of Archelaus's reign, as recorded by Josephus. It pays to take nothing for granted.

It is, I believe, also fair to say that the nativities recorded by both Matthew and Luke obviously reflect different evolving mythologies in different localities that had accumulated around Jesus after his execution. This phenomenon often, if not always, attached itself to significant personalities of the era, after their death or even before it. It could be considered that the length of time between the execution of Jesus and the writing of the Gospels was too short for the mythologizing process to have occurred to any great degree. However, there is modern evidence that it is entirely credible. The 'Cargo cults' that appeared in Melanesia and New Guinea just after the Second World War[12] were messianic in nature, and the cultures in which they occurred were probably at a similar level of technological development to that of the Holy Land in the first century CE. It has clearly been shown that these cults developed their own mythology within a normal lifetime from their origins.

We must now proceed in the hope that there are still elements of fact buried within both mythologies, and that one or more of these could be truly significant in uncovering the year of Jesus' birth. So we shall now consider the complete evidence for the birth of Jesus that is to be found in the Gospels of Matthew and Luke, by first of all considering:

The evidence of Matthew

So far all we have discovered from Matthew is that he placed Jesus' birth during the reign of Herod the Great: 40 to 4 BCE. But he does provide further information that could help reduce this range to a more useful one if we can extract the possible chronological evidence from the mythology, because he tells us of a star that stopped and a massacre that might not have been what it seems.

We shall begin, appropriately enough, by following:

The guiding star

There are those who believe that the 'guiding star' of Matthew's Gospel is just one of the elements of mythology that crept into the narrative of Jesus' life after his crucifixion.

---

12 See ch. 5 of Richard Dawkins's *The God Delusion* (2006), on 'Cargo cults'.

This might well prove to be so, but it is not my intention to eliminate any evidence without first examining it thoroughly and allowing the evidence itself to lead us to a conclusion on its validity.

Matthew tells us that the magi were drawn to Judaea by a star that they had followed 'from the east'. Most scholars seem to agree that the word magi, in this context, is probably best interpreted as astronomer/astrologer. People of that time were even more superstitious than they are today about unusual celestial activity, which they regarded as portents of great and terrible events. It was normal for them to try to find a terrestrial counterpart to explain, or be explained by, the sign in the sky.

The last twelve or so years of the first (or should it be called the last?) century BCE seem to have been quite a lively time for unusual celestial events. I have drawn the following list from a variety of sources:

12 BCE	Halley's comet
7 BCE	three separate conjunctions of Saturn and Jupiter in Pisces[13]
6 BCE	a conjunction of the planets Jupiter, Saturn and Mars
5 BCE	the 70-day nova or supernova[14]

For the third of these events I have found two sources: the *New Advent Catholic Encyclopaedia* website (Chronology of the life of Jesus Christ: absolute chronology: the Nativity) and the book *Jesus of Nazareth: The infancy narratives* (2012) by Joseph Ratzinger (aka Pope Benedict XVI). Both of these are

---

13 See www.public.iastate.edu/~lightandlife/triple. htm by Ashgrove, also Simo Parpola, 'The magi and the star', *Bible Review*, December 2001.

14 For further information consult 'Some notes on the visibility of the 5 BC Chinese star' on www.astrosurf.com/.../Star/Visibility_ Star.htm

secondary sources, but the second reveals that the originator of this data was Johannes Kepler (1571–1630 CE). Although this citation does not include a precise reference, as the author of the book was Pope Benedict XVI, I feel it is safe to assume that this is reliable. But, although Kepler was a brilliant astronomer and mathematician, I do not believe it was possible for anyone, in the 16th or 17th century CE, to have calculated *accurately* the relative positions of four planets, Jupiter, Saturn, Mars and Earth, 1,600 years or so earlier: he would simply have lacked the tools required.

Ratzinger also provides us with another interesting piece of information, for which he again gives no direct reference. He refers to the Austrian astronomer Konrad Ferrari d'Occhieppo (1907–2007), who apparently dismissed the nova (or supernova) from consideration while advocating that the conjunction of Jupiter and Saturn in Pisces was 'sufficient explanation' for the star of Bethlehem. The most polite thing I can say about this is that I find it baffling that neither d'Occhieppo nor Ratzinger deigned to share the former's reasoning with us, and consequently we shall reserve judgement until we have properly considered all of the options available.

Consideration of these last two paragraphs together seems to suggest that Ratzinger was pretty much on the fence when it came to identifying the guiding star. This is not a position that I find comfortable, so we shall proceed with our own efforts to determine which, if any, of these celestial events can be the one to which Matthew refers.

Matthew mentions 'the star' on three occasions. First he tells us that:

After his birth astrologers from the east arrived in Jerusalem, asking, 'Where is the child who is born to be king of the Jews? We observed the rising of his star, and we have come to pay him homage'

(Matthew 2: 1–2)

This is followed by:

> Herod next called the astrologers to meet him in private,
> and ascertained from them the time when the star had
> appeared.
>
> (Matthew 2: 7)

And lastly:

> They [the Magi] set out at the king's bidding; and the
> star which they had seen at the rising went ahead of them
> until it stopped, above the place where the child lay. At
> the sight of the star they were overjoyed.
>
> (Matthew 2: 7–10)

In these references Matthew requires the guiding star to
have been capable of rising, of appearing and of stopping.
So we must now consider whether it was possible for any of
the above celestial events to have given the impression to the
Magi that it was a star and that it did perform each of these
actions. We must do this in order to ascertain that Matthew's
record of these events could be factually correct, because if
it is not, then this information is worthless to this, and every
other, investigation.

The word 'star', in the first century BCE, covered a lot of
ground (or should that be sky?), but in general referred to
the celestial objects with 'fixed' relationships to each other.
Planets were familiar bodies known as wandering stars, and
comets were random, unpredictable and hence unwelcome,
visitors to our skies, probably also regarded as a kind of
wandering star. Conjunctions are not celestial objects but
celestial events: they are, from a terrestrial viewpoint, the
gradual drawing together of planets, wandering stars. They
are not that infrequent, and I find it inconceivable that any
astronomer or astrologer, even then, could possibly have
referred to a conjunction as a star. Although it is possible that
Matthew was capable of such a mistake, as he could not have
been a witness to any of these events, we can only assume that
his information came from another source and hope that the
source, and Matthew, recorded it accurately.

In astronomical terms the words 'rising', 'appearing' and 'stopping' suggest three specific events, although it can be argued that 'rising' is a special case of 'appearing'. In general terms, stars can be seen to 'rise' and 'set' every day. They can also 'appear', one way or another, but 'stopping' is another matter entirely. Nothing in the universe can ever be said to 'stop', in either an absolute or relative sense, so we will have to look very carefully at how celestial objects and events might *seem* to 'stop', from a terrestrial viewpoint.

- That we see celestial objects rising and setting is a product of the Earth's rotation. This is an everyday phenomenon, and although the reasons for it were not known in the first century BCE, people of that era were of course familiar with the sights themselves.
  - ∗ Wherever an observer is on the Earth's surface, they will see stars and planets rise and set. The only stars that do not rise and set are those that are very close to the celestial pole, like Polaris in the northern hemisphere, and Sigma Octantis in the southern, which seem instead to rotate about an invisible fixed point. All the planets are seen to rise and set because their paths through the sky are close to the celestial equator.
  - ∗ Conjunctions can rise and set as a whole, because they are made up of planets that seem to be in close proximity when viewed from Earth (and continue to appear so as they rotate).
  - ∗ Comets have very large and eccentric orbits about our Sun. They may also seem to rise and set while they are visible from our corner of the inner solar system.
  - ∗ Novas, because they are 'fixed' stars, will also rise and set unless they are close to a celestial pole. The nova of 5 BCE was close to the celestial equator, in the region between the constellations of Capricorn and Aquila, so it would have appeared to rise and set.
- Matthew's use of the word 'appear', when applied to each of our candidates for the guiding star, is capable of several interpretations:

* A fixed star near to the celestial pole, like Polaris, because it does not rise or set, gradually 'appears' in the sky as the sun sets and darkness falls, then 'disappears' at dawn as the light of the sun overpowers it.

* The nova of 5 BCE could be said to have appeared in the sky on 10 March and disappeared on 7 April. Of course, this is a figure of speech. The star was always present in the sky, but it seemed to 'appear' suddenly because of its hugely increased brightness when it went nova, and seemed to 'disappear' when that intense brightness ended with equal suddenness.

* Comets, by their very nature, also appear, remain visible for a while and then disappear again. Halley's comet is only visible to the naked eye from Earth for about three months of its seventy-four to seventy-nine-year orbit (since 240 BCE; currently seventy-five to seventy-six years), and yet for most of that time it is closer to Earth than the planet Pluto. Its emergence from out of the darkness of space in 12 BCE was a product of its proximity at that time; its appearance would have been gradual and might not have been noticed immediately.

* Conjunctions do not appear suddenly. They gradually and visibly 'assemble', then gradually and visibly 'disperse' over a period of weeks.

• The word 'stop' is the most difficult to interpret in the astronomical context. All celestial objects are in motion, both in an absolute sense and relative to every other celestial object. From our point of view on Earth the so-called fixed stars only seem to be stationary relative to each other, and seem to move across the sky because of planetary rotation. Those near the celestial equator move the fastest, relative to our vantage point, having an angular velocity of $0.25°$/minute. Two other considerations are pertinent here. First, for something to stop it must previously have been in motion. Second, if it stops, what happens to it afterwards?

* Polaris is the nearest thing to a 'stationary' object in the northern hemisphere, but it cannot be the guiding

star of Matthew's account, because it would have led the magi northwards.

* One very unusual scenario might fit Matthew's description. If a comet's angular velocity was closely matched with that of Earth while it was passing from west to east and close to the celestial equator, it would appear to gradually slow to a halt before continuing on its way. Its moment of 'stopping' might be imperceptible, but relative to the background of stars moving in the opposite direction, it could give the impression of being stationary, to a terrestrial observer, even when it is not. Frankly, I don't know if this is even possible, but it doesn't really matter because in order for this to happen the comet, before and after it appeared to have stopped, would have to move with the rotation of Earth, from west to east, which would have guided the magi in the wrong direction!

* Having considered all other possibilities, I am drawn to the conclusion that here Matthew must have been referring not to the cessation of motion but to the cessation of visibility. If this is so, only one of the significant celestial events fits the bill, and that is the nova. On or about 10 March 5 BCE, a hitherto unremarkable star, in the region between the constellations of Capricorn and Aquila, went nova. Its brightness suddenly increased so dramatically that it appeared as a new star, near the celestial equator,[15] in the skies of the Earth. It might have burned so brightly that it became visible in daylight. On or about 7 April 5 BCE, the star's fuel supply was used up, and as rapidly as it had appeared, its light dimmed and it disappeared from view. In other words, it stopped. To those who have English as their first language this may seem unlikely, as we do not usually apply the words 'starting' and 'stopping' to light. But this is not the case in all languages.

---

15 The celestial equator is a projection of the plane of the terrestrial equator onto the imaginary celestial sphere of outer space. SJD

From the reasoning above I believe that only one of the celestial events under consideration could have been the 'guiding star' of Matthew's account, and that is the nova of 5 BCE. It also seems quite reasonable that such a period of quite intense, and unusual, celestial activity, over a relatively short period of time could have been responsible for some kind of reaction among people in a relatively primitive society. However it is also necessary to point out that these astronomical phenomena were likely to have been visible over quite a large portion of the Earth's surface, and yet the only region for which there remains any evidence of such an extreme reaction is the kingdom of Judaea. So it is only right to ask ourselves why this was the case. Could it have been that there was an extra factor here that only had significance for the descendants of Israel, something that they associated specifically with the arrival of their Messiah? Perhaps.

The Jews of this era viewed the contents of the books that comprise the Torah, and also the Old Testament of the Christians' Holy Bible, not just as history, but also as a kind of guide book. When things were not going well for them, they would turn to their scrolls for inspiration and hope. They believed that every trial and tribulation of their present and future had been foreseen by the prophets of old, and that strategies and guidance resided within them as prophecies. Furthermore, there was at that time a long-unfulfilled prophecy, known as Balaam's oracle, that may explain their reaction:

> I see him but not now; I behold him, but not near; a star shall come forth out of Jacob, a comet arise from Israel.
> (Numbers 24: 17)

Given the remarkable similarity to the actual astronomical events that occurred in 12 BCE and 5 BCE, it isn't difficult to see how this quotation could have been seen as the fulfilment of Balaam's prophecy, and the actual events as a sign that the long-anticipated Messiah had at last been born, to reunite the twelve tribes and deliver them from what they saw as the tyranny of the Roman occupation. There were, however, a couple of problems here that needed to be overcome for people to have believed this.

First, the event at which this prediction was made occurred late in the lifetime of Moses, and shortly before the Children of Israel entered the Promised Land. A variety of different sources place the death of Moses between about 1,540 and 1,270 years before the events that this was supposed to foretell, which was, incidentally, also between 825 and 420 years before the founding of Rome!

Second, the context in which the prediction was made referred specifically to the struggle between the Israelites and the people indigenous to the Promised Land and its immediate vicinity, as the next part of the text clearly shows:

> He shall smite the squadrons of Moha, and beat down all the sons of strife. Edom shall be his by conquest and Seir, his enemy, shall be his.
>
> (Numbers 24: 17–18)

Last, this prophecy was made by Balaam, who was not a Jew and was probably pagan, and who caused the Moabites to triumph over the Israelites by 'wickedly' setting a trap for them. He:

> put temptation in the way of the Israelites. He encouraged them to eat food sacrificed to idols and to commit fornication ...
>
> (Revelation of John 2: 14–15)

The bait was taken and the Jews transgressed, which resulted in God sending them a deadly plague as punishment.

None of this would seem to recommend the reliability of Balaam's prophecy as the source of something as important to the Jews as the coming of their Messiah. Nevertheless it would appear that this was exactly what occurred. Surely it could only have been the coincidental similarities between Balaam's words and the celestial events of 12 BCE and 5 BCE that was responsible for this.

If this was indeed the case it would seem unlikely that the Jewish elders and priests knew exactly when the arrival of the Messiah would have been. It would only have been the last of these events, the guiding star, that finally persuaded them that the time of the Messiah had already arrived. There must have followed a time of great uncertainty and anticipation as they waited for the identity of the Messiah to be made known. And so it was.

There is a very strong possibility that each and every one of these celestial events had a part to play. The appearance of Halley's comet might have set the ball of Messianic anticipation rolling in 12 BCE, the conjunctions would have fuelled the flames in 7 and 6 BCE, and the nova of 5 BCE would have been seen to indicate that the prophecy was fulfilled and the Messiah had arrived. In that case anyone of the House of David with the right credentials is likely to have been considered a legitimate messianic candidate. Therefore, from this evidence, we have no choice other than to regard the year 12 BCE as the earliest possible year of Jesus' birth and 5 BCE as the latest possible year, unless the one remaining piece of evidence that Matthew has to offer provides us with something that allows us to narrow this range.

The massacre of the innocents

This event is referred to in only one historical document, the Gospel of Matthew. I find it difficult to believe that the brutal murder of all male children under the age of three in Bethlehem by the hated Herod the Great, for whatever reason, would have been forgotten so easily by the Jews, and the very fact that it is not recorded by Josephus is in itself strong, but not conclusive, evidence against its occurrence. Matthew tells us that:

> When Herod saw how the astrologers had tricked him he fell into a passion, and gave orders for the massacre of all children in Bethlehem and its neighbourhood, of the

age of two years or less, corresponding with the time he
had ascertained from the astrologers.

(Matthew 2: 16–17)

Matthew's account clearly states that, at the time when the
magi arrived in Jerusalem, 'the child who is born to be king of
the Jews' could have been up to two years of age (that is, less
than three years old), and not necessarily a new-born baby, at
least as far as Herod's advisers were concerned. But should
we give credence to the historicity of this event and use it to
help calculate the year of Jesus' birth? Yes,[16] but at this time
I believe we should treat it with a large degree of scepticism,
keep it in the back of our minds and consider any temporal
results that we draw from it as unreliable, unless and until we
discover corroboration for the event itself, or its date, from
other sources.

To this end it is worth considering another possibility:
that Matthew's 'massacre of the innocents' is based on a very
different event, for which there is independent evidence.
The creation of mythology is not a directed process and often
embraces other, unrelated events that may have occurred in
the same time-frame, draws them in and alters them along
the way. Such a process is clearly demonstrated in the way the
mythology of the Cargo Cults developed.

The event to which I refer here is Herod's execution of his
own sons, Aristobulus and Alexander (by his Hasmonean[17]
wife, Mariamne I), in 7 BCE.[18] (Because of the lack of

---

16 See Rule of Engagement no. 5.

17 The Hasmoneans (sometimes referred to as Hasmodeans) were
the last legitimate royal household of Israel, as far as the Jews were
concerned, before the Romans imposed the House of Herod on
them.

18 I have found this year given for the executions in several
chronologies and reference books, but each time without
provenance. I have found nothing in the works of Josephus to
enable us to corroborate it, and therefore believe it should be

provenance for this dating I must assign an error factor of +/-1 at least when using it.) This might seem too big a leap, especially as the sons were grown men at the time and not the innocent children of Matthew's narrative. However, the mythologizing process can certainly produce distortions of this scale. Curiously, fortuitously or just coincidentally, the year of these executions falls within the time range suggested by Matthew's other evidence.

If we employ this information as the First Gospel requires, there are two possible outcomes. The first suggests that the magi met Herod in 7 BCE +/-1, just prior to the executions, and that Jesus was born in one of the years from 11 to 6 BCE. The second suggests that if the nova of 5 BCE was 'the guiding star', the birth of Jesus occurred between then and 8 BCE, which encompasses the year of the executions, but in the wrong part of the narrative. But is this really significant? It is doubtful that many of those who contributed to the emerging mythology, in the middle of the first century BCE, would have either known the exact time and order of all these events or had the resources, or perhaps the will, to check them. Either way these are two intriguing possibilities, but they are not proof of anything.

In conclusion to this close look at Matthew's nativity evidence we can only say that there is a strong case for believing that Jesus was born at some time between, and inclusive of, the years **12 BCE and 5 BCE**.

The evidence of Luke

Of Luke and the fourth element

It would be useful at this juncture to find a way of eliminating Archelaus from consideration as the Herod mentioned by

---

regarded with a degree of caution. It will not be used here to date any other event.

Luke in connection with the nativity. I express it in this way as it is preferable here to have the reign of only one Herod to consider, and not two that are mutually exclusive. This may be made possible by consideration of two further gospel references, one of them Lucan, the other Johannine. The first of these says:

> When Jesus began his work he was about thirty years old.
> (Luke 3: 23)

Luke has here given us Jesus' age, albeit approximate, at an important event in his life: the beginning of his ministry. Should we not pay very special attention to someone who believed he knew the year of Jesus' birth *and* his age at a specific point in his life? After all, knowing the one would have allowed him to calculate or corroborate the other. So let us do the calculation for ourselves.

I shall take 'about thirty' to designate a five-year range, from the beginning of his 28th year to the end of the year of his 32nd birthday. This range is made up from his actual 30th year, the year of the 30th anniversary of his birth, and the second year of his being aged 30, plus a year either side for the 'about' word. Now, according to Luke (2: 1–2), Jesus was born at the time of a census conducted by Quirinius, and this census is also believed by many to have been the one taken by Quirinius on the deposition of Archelaus, as recorded by Josephus (*AJ*, book XVIII, ch. 1, para. 1), which places Jesus' birth in one of the years 5 to 7 CE.[19] For the moment it suits my purpose to leave this association unchallenged. If true, this would lead us to the range of possible years from 33 to 39 CE for the beginning of Jesus' ministry.

We also know, from all four of the Canonical Gospels, that Jesus was crucified during the governorship of Pontius Pilate, who presided at his trial. Pilate was governor of Judaea from 26 to 36 CE, which requires Jesus' ministry to have begun before

---

19 See 'The short reign of Herod Archelaus', page 40.

the Passover of 36 CE, the last year of Pilate's governorship, and hence the latest possible year for his execution of Jesus. This requires the very latest year that Jesus could have begun his ministry to be 36 CE. But, we also have to accommodate at least one more year, as the Fourth Gospel records another Passover between the beginning of Jesus' ministry and his execution. This leaves only the years 33 to 35 CE available for Jesus to have begun his ministry, and in these three years he would have been 26 at the youngest, and 30 at the oldest. This would just allow him to have been in his early thirties at the time of his execution, as Christian tradition holds, which is not perhaps an unexpected outcome.

The next reference we need to consider here is a rebuke that could have been made as late in Jesus' life as the year before his crucifixion. This is because, according to the Fourth Gospel, it occurred either at or just before a Festival of Dedication; the last festival to be mentioned before the last Passover of Jesus' life. As the Festival of Dedication is held in December, and the latest year possible for his crucifixion is the last year of Pilate's governorship, 36 CE, this make 35 CE the latest year possible for the following rebuke:

> The Jews protested, 'You [Jesus] are not yet fifty years old. How can you have seen Abraham?'
>
> (John 8: 57)

(Note: I will refer to this evidence in the future as the 'not yet 50 rebuke'.)

None other than Irenaeus[20] argued that had the intention of the Jews been to mock Jesus' youth, they would have

---

20 Irenaeus was born either between the years 115 and 125 CE or 130 and 142 CE. He was a Greek from Smyrna in Asia Minor and is believed to have been a student of Polycarp, also from Smyrna, who was raised as a Christian, rather than converting as an adult, became a priest and eventually succeeded the martyr Pothinus to become the second bishop of Lugdunum (modern-day Lyons) in Gaul.

accused him of being 'not yet 40 years old' if he had been only in his thirties at that time. So there is a valid implication that at the time the rebuke was made, Jesus was no younger than 41 and no older than 49. As we have just seen above, had Jesus been born in 6 CE (+/-1) he would have been between 28 and 30 years old in 35 CE. Can we honestly believe that 'you are not yet 50' would be a likely rebuke for a man of this age? Personally I think not, which leads me to believe that Jesus could not have been born in the years 6 CE (+/-1), when the census was taken by Quirinius on the deposition of Archelaus.

If we now apply the age range of 41 to 49 years to the year range we derived earlier, from Matthew, for the birth of Jesus, 12 to 5 BCE, we arrive at the following years for the 'not yet 50 rebuke': ([742 AUC + 41 =] 783 AUC to [749 AUC + 49 =] 798 AUC) 30 to 45 CE. This reduces to the years 30 to 36 CE when we allow for the governorship of Pilate, and to 30 to 35 CE when we allow for the latest possible year for the 'not yet 50 rebuke' being 35 CE.

Does this validate my contention, and that of Irenaeus, that the 'not yet 50 rebuke' implies that Jesus must have been in his forties at the time it was made? The answer to this question is 'no, not yet'. The reason is that it is also necessary for it to support the 'about 30 when he began his work' reference at the same time, and we cannot do this until we know exactly when his ministry began, from other sources. So for now, we shall have to suspend our judgement on this matter.

However unlikely it may seem at this stage of our investigation that we will be able to reconcile Luke's evidence with that of Matthew, we shall nevertheless continue to investigate each and every piece of evidence in a way that is open to the possibility of accommodation, or even reconciliation, between the nativities accorded to Matthew and Luke.

The time difference between the results we have so far derived from Matthew's evidence and Luke's is between nine and eighteen years. This is not insignificant, and it is at this point that many researchers dismiss Luke's nativity evidence, for a variety of reasons that I do not intend to pursue. I am more interested in following those opportunities that keep both Luke and Matthew 'in the game'. To this end I shall continue this investigation by considering some of the aspects of Luke's account that I mentioned in passing above in greater detail, while evaluating some other interesting hypotheses.

Of two censuses and two births

To begin with we shall look at an episode recorded by Luke in the Acts of the Apostles that also refers to a census. This incident occurred some time after Jesus' crucifixion, when some of his followers were 'taken before the Council' because they had been teaching in Jesus' name. When the mood of the Council became ugly and people began to call for the disciples' death, a Pharisee named Gamaliel advised caution, saying:

> Men of Israel, be cautious in deciding what to do with these men. Some time ago Theudas came forward … and … after him came Judas the Galilean at the time of the census; he induced some people to revolt under his leadership …

> (Acts of the Apostles 5: 33–37)

Here Luke requires Theudas to have preceded Judas of Galilee. Unfortunately in this he disagrees with Josephus,[21] who indicates that Theudas rose up under Fadus, the procurator in 45 or 46 CE, while he associates the revolt of Judas with the census taken on the deposition of Archelaus, 40 years earlier. We find that Luke's evidence presents us with a dilemma. However, I believe this instance clearly

---

21 *AJ,* book XX, ch. v, paras 1–4.

demonstrates that Luke was capable of making an error: he included an incorrect element in an account that is otherwise correct. He probably did so inadvertently, something that is not surprising considering the difficulties that must have existed for researchers of history at that still very primitive time. Even so, now we know that Luke did make one mistake it does not mean that every temporal reference he presents is wrong. It just emphasizes the need to proceed with caution when considering his evidence.

Perhaps more significant in this passage is the mention of the census. Was Luke here referring to the same census as that taken at the time of Jesus' birth, and if so, why did he not mention that association, as would have been natural? That he did not causes me to wonder if there might have been another, earlier census. I am by no means the first to have had this idea: Quintus Septimus Florens Tertullianus[22] (aka Tertullian) suggested a census conducted by Saturninus in 7 BCE, presumably because he too had problems reconciling the account given by Luke with that of Matthew.

In search of a lost census?

It should be noted here that many scholars regard this as a futile search. Dr Richard Carrier,[23] a noted expert on Roman history, for instance, claims that such a census could not have occurred, as if it had, there would be direct evidence of its existence. I'm afraid I have to disagree. There being no evidence of its existence is not proof that it did not occur, and if it did occur, might not the evidence of Luke be the only remaining evidence that it did so?

In those days a decree was issued by the Emperor

---

22 Tertullian (c. 160–225 CE) was an exponent of the Holy Trinity when it was a heresy. He is regarded as the father of Latin Christianity and the founder of western theology.

23 Richard Carrier, *Luke vs. Matthew on the Year of Christ's Birth* (2006).

Augustus for a registration to be made throughout the Roman world. This was the first registration of its kind; it took place when Quirinius was governor of Syria.

(Luke 2: 1–2)

This quotation provides us with four separate pieces of evidence. It is necessary to proceed by considering each of them singly, as well as in concert.

The reign of the Emperor Augustus

Gaius Octavius Thurinus became Gaius Julius Caesar Augustus, the first emperor of Rome, on 29 January 27 BCE, and died on 19 August 14 CE. This range is obviously so broad that it embraces the latter part of the reign of Herod the Great, all of the reign of Archelaus and the census of Quirinius in 6 CE, and does not help us in any way.

The life of Quirinius

Publius Sulpicius Quirinius was born in the region of Lanuvium, a town near Rome, of an undistinguished though wealthy family. Quirinius followed the normal pathway of service for an ambitious young man of his social class. In 15 BCE, Augustus appointed him as governor with the rank of proconsul of the province of Crete and Cyrenaica. There he subdued the Nasamones, a native tribe. Then, according to the Roman historian Florus, Quirinius defeated the Garamantes (or Marmaridae), a tribe of the Sahara desert from Cyrenaica, possibly while still governor of Crete and Cyrene, around 14 BCE. In 12 BCE he was elected consul, a sign that he enjoyed the favour of Augustus. Some years later, he led a campaign against the Homonadenses, a tribe based in the mountainous region of Galatia and Cilicia, around 5 to 3 BCE, probably while he was legate of Galatia and Pamphylia. He won by reducing their strongholds and starving out the defenders. For this victory he was awarded a triumph. By 1 CE Quirinius was appointed rector to Augustus's grandson Gaius Caesar, until the latter died from wounds suffered on campaign, in 3 CE. When Augustus's support shifted to his stepson Tiberius, Quirinius followed by joining his camp, soon after which he was appointed governor of Syria, one of the most important provinces of the empire, garrisoned with no less than four legions.

After the banishment of Archelaus, greater Iudaea (Samaria, Judaea and Idumea) came under direct Roman administration, with Coponius as prefect, and Quirinius was instructed to assess Iudaea province for taxation purposes. One of his first duties was to carry out a census as part of this. The Jews already hated their pagan conquerors, and censuses were forbidden under Jewish law. The assessment was greatly resented by the Jews, and open revolt was prevented only by the efforts of the high priest Joazar. As it was, the census did trigger the revolt of Judas of Galilee and the formation of the party of the Zealots, according to Josephus. Quirinius served as governor of Syria with nominal authority over Iudaea until 12 CE, when he returned to Rome as a close associate of Tiberius. He died in 21 CE and was given a public funeral.

It is of more than passing interest that from this brief biography there appears to be a gap in our knowledge of Quirinius's whereabouts and activities between the years 12 and 3 BCE. These years fall right in the middle of the period of time towards which Matthew's Gospel has already directed us for news of Jesus' birth.

Registration throughout the Roman world

According to Josephus:

> Now Cyrenius ... came at this time into Syria ... being sent by Caesar to be a judge of that nation, and to take an account of their substance. Coponius also, a man of the equestrian order, was sent together with him, to have the supreme power over the Jews. Moreover, Cyrenius came himself into Judea, which was now added to the province of Syria, to take an account of their substance, and to

dispose of Archelaus's money; but the Jews, although at the beginning they took the report of a taxation heinously, yet did they leave off any further opposition to it, by the persuasion of Joazar, who was the son of Beethus, and high priest; so they, being over-persuaded by Joazar's words, gave an account of their estates, without any dispute about it. Yet was there one Judas, a Gaulonite, of a city whose name was Gamala, who, taking with him Sadduc, a Pharisee, became zealous to draw them to a revolt, who both said that this taxation was no better than an introduction to slavery, and exhorted the nation to assert their liberty; as if they could procure them happiness and security for what they possessed, and an assured enjoyment of a still greater good, which was that of the honour and glory they would thereby acquire for magnanimity.

(Josephus, *AJ* book XVIII, ch. 1, p. 1)

Luke mentions no date, of course. It is the association of Quirinius with the census in the account of the nativity in his gospel, together with the association of Quirinius and the census taken after the deposition of Archelaus, according to Josephus in *Antiquities of the Jews,* that produces the link. But is this justified? In his gospel Luke mentions nothing about the deposition of Archelaus, nor does he refer to the unrest and resentment caused by the imposition of this census that Joazar tried to quell and which led to the revolt of Judas of Galilee, although he does mention it in the Acts without reference to the birth of Jesus, as we have seen earlier.

The major stumbling block here is that Quirinius was governor of Syria only once, from 6 to 12 CE. Admittedly there is room in the gaps in our knowledge of his biography to allow him to have been governor of Syria before, and at the right time, but there is also strong evidence against this. For a start there is no record that any Roman official was ever appointed governor of the same province twice. Presumably it would have been seen as a retrograde step, and had it ever occurred, the official concerned would surely have received some attention from Roman historians. Furthermore, it is known that other Roman officials held this position during this period: Marcus Vespanius Agrippa, 23 to 13 BCE; Marcus Titius, 13 or 12 BCE to 10 or 9 BCE; Gaius Sentius Saturninus, 10 or 9 BCE to 7 or 6 BCE; Publius Quinctilius Varus, 7 or 6 BCE to 4 BCE.

But this does not mean that all of Luke's evidence relating to the birth of Jesus is wrong, and it does not mean that there cannot have been another, earlier census in the later years of Herod the Great's reign, with which either Luke mistakenly associated Quirinius, or his actual involvement was different from being governor of Syria: such as *legatus ad census accipiendos*,[24] perhaps.

Another possibility here is that it was a case of mistaken identity. Above we can see that Publius Quinctilius Varus was governor of Syria from 7 or 6 BCE to 4 BCE. Is it possible that Luke confused Publius Quinctilius with Publius Quirinius because of the similarity of their names? It would be a very understandable error. There is a large 'but' here, however, as Publius Quinctilius Varus became infamous in 9 CE when the army of three legions that he commanded was not just defeated but massacred by Germanic tribesmen in the battle of Teutoberg Forest. It was one of the heaviest defeats ever suffered by the Roman army, after which the disgraced Varus did the 'honourable thing' and committed suicide. The fact that the story of Varus's disgrace would probably have been well known seems to reduce the possibility of Luke confusing him with someone else only about 60 years later, although it does not make it impossible.

One other piece of evidence could be relevant here. A stone now known as the Lapis Tiburtinus was found about half a mile from the doorstep of Quinctilius Varus's villa at Tibur (modern-day Tivoli), and now resides in the Vatican Museum. Its inscription eulogises the career of a high-ranking Roman, and may claim that he was legate or governor of Syria

---

24 This basically means 'legate in charge of taking censuses'.

twice. There is disagreement over the identity of the Roman, with different authorities claiming Sentius Saturninus, Publius Quinctilius Varus and Publius Sulpicius Quirinius. Given where it was found I have difficulty believing the stone refers to anyone other than Varus without direct evidence to the contrary. I also find the discussion regarding the meaning of the word *iterum* in the inscription – either 'twice' or 'second' – inconclusive. But this could well be evidence that there was at least one case of a Roman official occupying the governorship of Syria twice, even though this does not appear in the lists.

None of this is definitive, but let us explore further the possibility that Luke and Josephus were talking about two different censuses. Luke's reference was to 'the first registration of its kind' and Josephus's reference was to the one taken after the banishment of the ethnarc Herod Archelaus. This might have been more likely if Luke completed his Gospel before Josephus produced his *Antiquities of the Jews*, but it is not clear whether this was the case.

Let us consider the *Res Gestae Divi Augusti*,[25] a somewhat pompous valediction, composed by the Emperor Augustus himself. Within it he recorded the introduction of his censuses in paragraph 8:

When I was consul the fifth time [29 BCE], I increased the number of patricians by order of the people and senate. I read the roll of the senate three times, and in my sixth consulate [28 BCE] I made a census of the people with Marcus Agrippa as my colleague. I conducted a lustrum, after a forty-one year gap, in which lustrum were counted 4,063,000 heads of Roman citizens. Then again, with consular imperium I conducted a lustrum alone when Gaius Censorinus and Gaius Asinius were consuls [8 BCE], in which lustrum were counted 4,233,000 heads of Roman citizens. And the third time, with consular imperium,

25 See http://classics.mit.edu/Augustus/deeds.html for the full text.

I conducted a lustrum with my son Tiberius Caesar as colleague, when Sextus Pompeius and Sextus Apuleius were consuls [14 BCE], in which lustrum were counted 4,937,000 of the heads of Roman citizens. By new laws passed with my sponsorship, I restored many traditions of the ancestors, which were falling into disuse in our age, and myself I handed on precedents of many things to be imitated in later generations.[26]

The most striking feature of this is that there is no reference to a census anywhere in 6 CE, the year of the Syrian census recorded by Josephus. It is also significant that no places are mentioned. This leads me to believe that Augustus was recording censuses conducted in the same locality over a forty-two-year period, as the numbers seem to reflect normal growth, and that the place was probably the Italian peninsula. (Whether this is the case is not vital to the overall argument being made here.) The major point is, however, that as Augustus did not record the census in Syria of 6 CE, it cannot be taken for granted that any of the dates Augustus mentioned refer to another, otherwise unknown census in Syria or Judaea.

So could there have been a census conducted by either Quirinius or Quinctilius between about 15 and 4 BCE? Certainly it is conceivable, because there is a gap in our knowledge of the whereabouts of Quirinius between the year of his consulship, 12 BCE, and his leading the campaign against the Homonadenses, at some time during the years of 5 to 3 BCE. This gap in our knowledge of Quirinius's life also contains the years during which Quinctilius was governor of Syria (7 to 4 BCE) and is overlapped by the range of years suggested for the birth of Jesus by the celestial activity we have identified from Matthew's Gospel (12 to 5 BCE). But these remain interesting coincidences at the moment, and not yet proof of an earlier Judaean census.

26 All of the dates in this translation of the *Res Gestae* suggest consular references, but these were not present on the original *lapis,* so they must be regarded with caution.

There is another ancient fragment of information that may be of some relevance here, which is known as the Lapis Venetus. This is the tombstone of one Q. Aemilius Secundus, a low-ranking Roman officer who listed his achievements, including the conducting of a census at Apamea (a city in Syria) under the authority of Publius Sulpicius Quirinius. The date of the stone is not known, so it is not unreasonable to assume that the census referred to is the one taken on the deposition of Archelaus. That assumption, of course, does no more than help to confirm what we already think we know. But there are other scholars with a different view of this. They would have us believe that there are 'microletters' on this stone that lead to a quite different conclusion. I put it this way as I have as yet not found any independent evidence of the existence of these 'microletters'. To the best of my knowledge there are no photographs, although if the claimants want us to take them seriously, these might be thought essential to their cause.

But if there were photographs we would apparently see the legend 'LA CONS P.S. QVIRINI'. This these scholars translate as 'Year One of the Consulship of P. S. Quirinius', which leads them to the conclusions that Quirinius conducted a census in Syria during his consular year, and that this could have been the census of the nativity referred to by Luke, and therefore the year of Jesus' birth. They may be right, but unfortunately seeing is believing. Also, although I am no expert on Roman history, I would have thought that this unlikely to have been a task for someone in his consular year.

I believe that the Lapis Venetus does nothing more than confirm what we already know from Josephus: that a census was conducted in Syria by Quirinius after the deposition of Archelaus.

The first of its kind

This phrase in Luke's reference is usually taken to mean 'the first of a series'. However, this too is something that bears reconsideration. Could it have meant rather that this census was different from every other census that had preceded it, and if so, in what way could it have been different? The most obvious answer is that the difference lay in the requirement for each and every person and family to return 'to his own town' for the registration. But there might be another, completely different reason.

Many scholars of this period of Roman and Jewish history are adamant that a second, earlier census could not have occurred. Their reasoning is both logical and forceful. Herod was an ally of Augustus who looked after Iudaea on his behalf. The kingdom was neither taxed nor administered by Rome until 6 CE, and imposing a census over Herod's head would only have antagonized him and undermined his authority. There would be little to gain by doing so and much to lose. Augustus would have been a fool to do so.

Although these arguments make sense, it is perhaps going too far to suggest that Roman emperors never made decisions that were improbable and ill-advised. They had a habit of being arrogant and ruthless, and were quite capable of being reckless. It is much more certain that if Augustus had implemented such a measure he must have thought he had very strong reasons to do so, and the resulting census would have been the first, and possibly the only, one of its kind. What is required here is evidence that Augustus had a reason to do so during the reign of Herod the Great, and there is just a chance that Josephus has provided us with this reason. It would appear that Augustus took an extremely dim view of a war conducted by Herod against the 'Arabs', to the extent that, according to Josephus, the emperor:

> ... wrote to Herod sharply. The sum of his epistle was this, that whereas of old he had used him as his friend, he should now use him as his subject.
>
> (*AJ* vol. XVI, ch. ix, para. 3)

Before this incident, Josephus goes to great lengths to stress the good favour in which Augustus held Herod; after it, he stresses the lengths to which Augustus went to distance himself from their earlier friendship, by refusing to receive gifts, letters and envoys from Herod. However, we are only concerned with whether the emperor's revenge on his ex-friend extended to the indignity of a census on his kingdom, and if so, whether it could have occurred within the date range we have already determined for the birth of Jesus.

Josephus does not say directly when the schism occurred, but he does provide us with information that brackets it. He presents the following events in this order, as can be seen by the references:

- Herod's sons, Aristobulus and Alexander, return from Rome (*AJ*, book XVI, ch. i, paras 1–2).
- Augustus reduces Herod to subject status (*AJ*, book XVI, ch. ix, para. 3).
- Augustus and Herod are reconciled (*AJ*, book XVI, ch. x, para. 9).
- Herod executes Aristobulus and Alexander (*AJ*, book XVI, ch. xi, para. 7).

Aristobulus IV and his brother Alexander lived most of their lives outside of Judaea, having been sent to Rome to be educated at the Imperial court, at ages 12 and about 16 respectively, in 20 BCE.[27] The young brothers returned to Jerusalem in 12 BCE and were apparently received enthusiastically by the populace. After many failed attempts at reconciliation between the king and his sons and heirs, the sick and by that time somewhat demented Herod had Aristobulus and Alexander strangled to death on charges of treason in 7 BCE. Herod then raised his first-born son, Antipater II, to co-regent and heir apparent. Incidentally it was at this time that Augustus made his famous remark that it was safer to be one of Herod's pigs than one of his sons.

This could indicate that if Augustus had ordered a census

---

27 All references to the years in which Aristobulus IV and Alexander were sent to Rome, returned from Rome and were executed, have been presented without provenance wherever I have encountered them. They therefore have to be treated with caution.

in reprisal for Herod's alleged disloyalty, it would have been taken during one of the years between 12 and 7 BCE. This lies comfortably in the date range we have derived for the birth of Jesus from Matthew's Gospel, overlaps the years during which the whereabouts of Quirinius were unknown, and might just include the first year of Quinctilius's governorship of Syria. It would also have preceded the deaths of Alexander and Aristobulus, and does not preclude the possibility that their brutal executions were the origin of Matthew's 'massacre of the innocents'.

- Possible years for a lost census: 12 to 7 BCE
- The execution of Alexander and Aristobulus: 7 +/- 1 BCE
- The guiding star: the nova of 5 BCE

However, if this census had occurred we might expect to find it recorded by Josephus. But it is by no means certain that because Josephus did not record it, it absolutely could not have happened: after all, Josephus also made no mention at all of Jesus.[28] It is an intriguing possibility that Luke's account is the only evidence remaining of this census.

We cannot at this point claim to have proved that there was a census taken in this place and this period of time that has since been (almost?) lost to history. What we can say is that there is nothing that absolutely excludes it. Meanwhile we must wait to see whether anything we discover later in this investigation either refutes or confirms it.

The two-nativities hypotheses: grasping at straws?

Here we shall consider what are either two hypotheses or a single hypothesis that exists in two different forms, both of

---

28 That is if we accept the current belief that the one reference to Jesus in Josephus is a later addition.

which have been suggested by other researchers also attempting to reconcile the accounts of the nativities given by Matthew and Luke, but without requiring another, earlier census.

Of two babies

This hypothesis is both difficult to prove and difficult to refute. It is this: that Matthew was recording the birth of John the Baptist and Luke that of Jesus. This could work provided we were prepared to accept that Matthew could have mistaken John's birth for that of Jesus. It might seem improbable, but let us consider what it would entail.

Matthew's account could not realistically have been based on John's birth unless John was born in Bethlehem. This is because there is a passage in the Torah which also appears in the Old Testament, that many Jews of the time believed was a 'prophecy' concerning the expected Messiah. It requires him to be born in Bethlehem and, by implication, to be of the House of David. It is this:

> But you, Bethlehem in Ephrathah, small as you are to be among Judah's clans, out of you shall come forth a governor for Israel, one whose roots are far back in the past, in days gone by.
>
> (Micah 5: 2)

However there is no claim in the New Testament that the Baptist was of the Davidic line. Luke tells us that when Mary, at some time after her encounter with Gabriel, visited her kinswoman Elizabeth and her husband Zechariah, while the former was carrying John, she 'went straight away to a town in the uplands of Judah' (Luke 1: 39). Bethlehem is, of course, a town in the uplands of Judaea.

It is a common assumption that Luke's Gospel indicates that Mary conceived Jesus before she visited Elizabeth, and that Jesus was born about six months after John. However, at no time does Luke say anything concerning when Mary conceived. After recording the birth of John Luke gives a brief biography of him, from his birth to his first 'public appearance', presumably at Bethania, as we shall see shortly. He immediately follows this by relating the birth of Jesus. If the visit of Gabriel to Mary was connected to her betrothal to Joseph, as seems likely, the messenger might have been explaining that hers was a dynastic marriage, one intended, by mixing her blood-line with that of the House of David, to produce a candidate for the throne of Israel. Mary was informed of this in the sixth month of Elisabeth's pregnancy, went immediately to visit her and stayed for three months, leaving presumably either immediately before or just after the birth of John. This allows a lot of leeway for the time of the conception, and therefore allows us to conclude that there is nothing in Luke's Gospel to contradict the two-nativities hypothesis.

However, if Matthew was recording John's birth, how can we explain his references to Mary and Joseph, the 'immaculate conception', the conception being out of wedlock, and Joseph having cold feet because of it? This would require Matthew to have 'known' the circumstances of Jesus' conception and birth, and to have attached them, wholesale, to the date and place of John's birth. This is neither impossible nor even improbable, but it is difficult to see how it can be either confirmed or dismissed.

This hypothesis was originally suggested, I believe, to justify the argument that the year of the Quirinian census, 6 CE, was also that of Jesus' birth. We have already seen that it is extremely improbable that Jesus was born at this time, which in my view renders this solution to the problem of the two nativity accounts even more improbable. But there is another possible explanation that is also dependent on two births and might just about explain everything.

Of two births

There is an episode of Jesus' life that is narrated in only one Gospel, that of Luke, which could just be the clue to solving this entire problem. It is this:

> Now it was the practice of his parents to go to Jerusalem
> every year for the Passover festival; and when he was
> twelve, they made the pilgrimage as usual.
>
>   (Luke 2: 41–42)

To Jews, then as now, the thirteenth year is significant.[29] It is
the age at which a boy becomes a man, and the celebration of
this event, today called Bar Mitzvah, is a major one in Jewish
life. It is thought by some that the Jews of this time regarded
the 'coming of age' as a symbolic second birth.[30] Luke, having
been a gentile convert to Christianity, might have had limited
knowledge of the niceties of Judaism, knowing some things and
not knowing others. Having only fragments of Jesus' life with
which to work, plus the growing mythology that was beginning
to obscure the truth of events, he did the best he could.

Is it possible that it was the passing of Jesus' twelfth birthday
that occasioned his visit to Jerusalem, at Passover, as part of
his symbolic 'rebirth', which took place in the year of the
Quirinian census on the deposition of Archelaus in 5 to 7 CE?
If so this indicates that he was born between 9 and 6 BCE, which
in turn would have made him 30 in 22 to 25 CE and 41 in 33 to
36 CE! This conforms with all of the pertinent dating evidence
that we have so far discovered in the Gospels, and does not
require an earlier, unrecorded census, although it still allows
for there to have been one.

It also does something else. It allows for the nativity
accorded to Matthew and the nativity accorded to Luke to
coexist without the inherent contradictions being glossed over,
as in the consensus. This is because it *requires* the events given
by Luke to follow after those given by Matthew. Matthew says
that after the birth Joseph and family went to Egypt to avoid

29 The important age for this rite of passage is sometimes referred
to as being at the age of 12 and sometimes as being in the 13th
year: as I showed earlier in 'Trouble with time', this is because
when people are 12 years old they are in their 13th year.

30 Barbara Thiering, *Jesus the Man* (1993), p. 67.

the 'massacre of the innocents', then after Herod's death, they *settled* in Nazareth because they were afraid to *return* to Bethlehem because of Archelaus's accession. Luke says that after Jesus' 'birth', in the year of Archelaus' deposition, they *returned* to their home village of Nazareth. This explanation requires no earlier census and makes perfect sense. But is this all just too good to be true? Possibly.

Summary of the nativity evidence

This suggests the following timeline for the birth of Jesus and related events:

40 or 39 BCE	Herod the Great's accession *de jure*
38 to 36 BCE	Herod the Great's accession *de facto*
12 BCE	**Earliest possible year for Jesus' birth suggested by Matthew's evidence**
12 BCE	Appearance of Halley's comet
12 BCE	Herod's sons return from Rome
12 BCE	Earliest possible year for the 'lost census'
11 BCE	Gap in the record of Quirinius begins here
8 BCE	Earliest year for execution of Herod's sons
7 BCE	Three separate conjunctions of two planets in Pisces
7 BCE	Usual year assigned for execution of Herod's sons
7 BCE	Earliest year for Quinctilius to have been governor of Syria
7 BCE	**Latest possible year for Jesus' birth (from the 'not yet 50' rebuke)**
7 BCE	Latest possible year for the 'lost census'
6 BCE	Possible conjunction of three planets
6 BCE	Latest year for execution of Herod's sons
5 BCE	Appearance of the 70-day nova! The guiding star?
5 BCE	Gap in the record of Quirinius ends here
5 BCE	**Latest possible year for Jesus' birth suggested by Matthew's evidence**

| 4 BCE | Death of Herod the Great: Archelaus becomes ethnarc of Judaea |
| 5 to 7 CE | Archelaus deposed, the census of Quirinius and possibly the year in which Jesus was at Jerusalem for Passover, at the age of 12. |

The two years of **40 and 39 BCE** we have derived for Herod's accession *de jure* are fairly secure, and will be used elsewhere when required. The three years derived for his accession *de facto* were found by adding the elapsed time of three years to his accession *de jure*, so they need not and will not be used in any further calculations unless it is absolutely essential.

The range of years derived for the 'lost census' is viable, but this does not prove that this census occurred. This range of years will not be used in further calculations.

The range of years suggested for the execution of Herod's sons does not prove that this event was the origin of the 'massacre of the innocents', and will not be used in any further calculations.

The year **4 BCE** is generally regarded as the date of the death of Herod the Great, and our investigation has confirmed this. This date is safe to use in future calculations.

For the census conducted by Quirinius on the deposition of Archelaus we have the range from **5 to 7 CE**. Although Archelaus was most probably deposed in **6 CE**, as I have shown, this does not necessarily require the census to have been taken in the same year.

Application of the 'about 30 when he began his work' reference, from Luke's Gospel, to the year range for the census suggests it is possible for one of these years to have been the birth year of Jesus. Application of the 'not yet 50' rebuke, from the Fourth Gospel, to the date range for the census suggests that all of these years are too late to have been the birth year of Jesus. When considered together these two references exclude the year of this census from being the birth year of Jesus.

This summary is not yet definitive, as we cannot exclude the possibility that something we discover later in this investigation will change our understanding of the way and the time that these events occurred. So we must continue to keep an open mind when we move on to our consideration of the evidence for the beginnings of Jesus' public life and his ministry.

Cometh the hour, cometh the man?

As I progressed through the investigation of the nativity evidence a thought began to nag away at me. Is it probable that around 5 BCE the Messianic arrival the Jews had been anticipating would be in the form of a baby? Of course he would have been born a baby, but would the association of Balaam's predicted celestial activity, real or metaphorical, have been expected to signify the arrival of a baby or a man? I find it hard to imagine the Jews getting wildly excited that the Messiah had been born if they would then have to wait about thirty years for him to liberate them.

If anticipation of the arrival of the Messiah was initiated by the appearance of Halley's comet in 12 BCE, and the flames of Messianic fervour were fanned by the conjunctions of 7 BCE, and possibly that of 6 BCE, then the nova of 5 BCE would surely have convinced many Jews that the prophecy of Balaam was in the process of being fulfilled. So surely they were expecting a man to step out of obscurity, seize the moment, unite the tribes and lead them to victory over the Romans. A man like Judas of Galilee, perhaps, who was to some a Messianic candidate.

After Judas's failure showed him to have been a false Messiah, however, the Jews must have been downhearted and bewildered by the lack of the true Messiah. Surely it was at about this time that they would have begun to look for alternative interpretations of the events in order to keep their hope for the fullfilment of the prophecy alive. That new interpretation may well be the origin of the nativity mythologies provided by Luke and Matthew, which were perhaps not even written down until after Jesus' execution. That a candidate who met the criteria of age, place of birth and lineage was actively being sought by the Jews at the time that John the Baptist proclaimed Jesus is, however, a matter of record.

Of two beginnings

The consensus – Part 2

Consensus sequence	Matt	Mark	Luke	John
John appears in or from the wilderness	3:1	1:4	3:2	1:6
John baptises at Bethania-over-Jordan	3:5	1:4	3:3	1:28
Jesus begins his public life when ...				
... John baptises him at Bethania and ...	**3:15**	**1:9**	**3:21**	
...the 'dove' descends upon him	**3:16**	**1:10**	**3:22**	**1:32**
Jesus is tempted in the wilderness	4:1	1:12	4:2	
Jesus recruits his first disciples				*1:35*
Jesus goes to the wedding at Cana				*2:1*
Jesus visits Capharnaum				*2:12*
First Passover of Jesus' public life				*2:13*
Jesus meets Nicodemus				*3:1*
Jesus and John go to Aenon to baptise				*3:22*
John is arrested	4:12	1:14	3:20	
Jesus begins his ministry	**4:17**	**1:15**	**3:33**	

There may be slight variations in the way the way the consensus is perceived by some, but I believe that this table encapsulates the most frequently found sequence of events assumed by it.

The insertion of the unique section of the Fourth Gospel (highlighted in italics) within the narrative provided by the Synoptics is not the only accommodation required here to produce the consensus. I shall list the others briefly, as I shall discuss them in greater detail later in this investigation:

- The baptism of Jesus by John is not recorded in the Fourth Gospel.
- The temptation of Jesus in the wilderness is not recorded in the Fourth Gospel.
- The author of the Fourth Gospel neither expresses an opinion nor clearly demonstrates when, or where in the sequence of events, Jesus began his ministry.
- The Fourth Gospel does not allow us to position accurately the moment of John the Baptist's arrest in the sequence of events. But it does imply that he was arrested either at, or shortly after, the baptism at Aenon, when it says:

> John too was baptising at Aenon, near to Salim … This was before John's imprisonment.
>
> (John 3: 22–24)

The order of some of the important events given in Luke's Gospel also differs from that shown in the other Synoptics, as can be seen clearly from the numbering of the Lucan references in the table above. The consensus does not resolve this. It is for this reason that I believe we must not treat Luke as 'synoptic' with Matthew and Mark in this particular, and should pay careful attention to what he tells us and how and when he tells it to us.

The two events highlighted in bold text in the consensus are those events for which we shall try to derive dates in this part of our investigation: the 'beginning of his public life' and the 'beginning of his ministry'.

The table clearly shows that Matthew and Mark must have believed that the 'public life of Jesus' began at Bethania and his ministry began after the arrest of John the Baptist. The author of the Fourth Gospel also demonstrates that Jesus' public life began at Bethania, but says nothing that suggests or demonstrates either where or when his ministry actually began. It could have been at Bethania, at the wedding at Cana, at Capharnaum, at the first Passover of his public life at Jerusalem, or before, at, or some time shortly after the baptisms at Aenon.

Only one of the Evangelists makes specific mention of Jesus beginning his ministry, and that is Luke.

> When Jesus began his work he was about thirty years old.
> (Luke 3: 23)

We shall now consider these two key events in the life of Jesus separately.

The beginning of his public life

This is relatively simple to define: it is the moment that we first meet Jesus as an adult. Establishing exactly when and where that moment occurred is also relatively simple to determine, as all four Gospels place the moment at a general baptism conducted by John the Baptist. This is the only baptism mentioned in each of the Synoptic Gospels, and the first baptism mentioned in the Fourth Gospel, and placed by it at Bethania-beyond-Jordan.

The reason we know this is that the Evangelists all have John introducing Jesus in much the same way. Mark's version is:

> It happened at this time that Jesus came from Nazareth, in Galilee, and was baptised in the Jordan by John. At the moment when he came up out of the water, he saw the heavens torn open and the Spirit, like a dove, descending upon him.
>
> (Mark 1: 9–10)

Similar accounts are given at Matthew 3: 13–16 and Luke 3: 21–22. The Fourth Gospel, although it does not mention John baptising Jesus, describes a similar incident at the first baptism, at Bethania:

> I saw the Spirit coming down from heaven like a dove and resting upon him.
>
> (John 1: 32–33)

This clearly establishes that the one baptism recorded by the Synoptics is the first one recorded in the Fourth Gospel and placed at Bethania. Therefore, this is where, and when, Jesus became a public figure, and hence began his public life.

The beginning of his ministry

This beginning also seems to be quite easy to identify. Mark and Matthew clearly demonstrate this by the sequence of events they give in their gospels. Mark has:

> Thereupon the Spirit sent him away into the Wilderness .... After John had been arrested Jesus came into Galilee proclaiming the Gospel of God: 'The time has come; the Kingdom of God is upon you, repent and believe the Gospel.'
>
> (Mark 1: 12–15)

While Matthew says:

> Jesus was then led away into the wilderness ...
>
> (Matthew 4: 1)

> When he heard that John had been arrested Jesus withdrew to Galilee.
>
> (Matthew 4: 12)

> From that day Jesus began to proclaim the message:
> 'Repent, for the Kingdom of Heaven is upon you.'
>
> (Matthew 4: 17)

We can only conclude from this that, as far as Mark and Matthew were concerned, the ministry of Jesus began almost immediately after the arrest of John.

But the Fourth Gospel makes it clear that the period of time between the baptism at Bethania and the arrest of John was considerably longer than it appears to have been in the Synoptics. From this we must conclude that the beginning of the public life of Jesus was separated from the beginning of his ministry by a period of some months, as according to the consensus he had to journey from Bethania-beyond-Jordan to Cana-in-Galilee for the wedding, go on to Capharnaum, travel to Jerusalem for the Passover, and then move on to Aenon for the second baptism, before returning to Galilee to begin his ministry after the arrest of John. That was quite a schedule, especially considering it was probably travelled on foot.

Bearing this in mind, we can now take on the task of trying to apply the evidence available to date each of these two significant events in the life of Jesus. We shall begin by:

Following the consensus

The first reference we need to consider here comes from Luke's Gospel:

> In the fifteenth year of the Emperor Tiberius, when Pontius Pilate was governor of Judaea, when Herod was prince of Galilee, his brother Philip prince of Ituraea and Trachonitis, and Lysansias prince of Abilene, during the high-priesthood of Annas and Caiaphas, the word of God came to John son of Zachariah in the Wilderness.
>
> (Luke 3: 1–3)

The first time we encountered this Lucan fanfare of the famous, only the years 13 and 14 CE were considered as possible years for the accession of Tiberius (see page 39). The first was the year he was made co-emperor with Augustus and the second the year of Augustus's death, when Tiberius became the sole and absolute ruler of the Rome Empire. There is no good reason to do otherwise here.

These accession dates lead us to the three possible years of 27 to 29 CE for the fifteenth year of his reign. The years in which Pontius Pilate was governor of Judaea are generally accepted to have been 26 to 36 CE, although some scholars claim he did not leave Judaea until early in 37, albeit before the Passover. The remainder of the reference here seems neither to contradict nor to narrow the range given by the fifteenth year of Tiberius. We can therefore claim with reasonable confidence that the event to which this passage is believed to refer, the emergence of John the Baptist from the wilderness, occurred in one of the three years from **27 to 29 CE**.

The second reference to consider is one that comes from the Fourth Gospel. This has only indirect associations with both the beginning of Jesus' public life and the beginning of his ministry, as it occurs between the baptism at Bethania and the arrest of John: it concerns the first Passover of Jesus' public life.

> 'Destroy the temple,' Jesus replied, 'and in three days I will raise it again.' They said, 'It has taken forty-six years to build this temple'...
>
> (John 2: 19–20)

We can identify when the rebuilding of the Temple began from two references provided by Josephus, although they do not seem to support each other.

> ... in the fifteenth year of his reign, Herod rebuilt the temple.
>
> (*JW*, book I, ch. xxi, para. 1)

> ... now Herod, in the eighteenth year of his reign ...
> undertook ... to build of himself the temple of God.
>
> (*AJ*, book XV, ch. xi, para. 1)

Inconveniently Josephus has once again given us two different periods of elapsed time relative to an event, and he does not clarify whether the starting year for these periods was that of Herod's accessions *de jure* or *de facto*. Some scholars claim that Josephus made a mistake in *Jewish Wars* that he corrected in *Antiquities of the Jews*. Surely the most likely reason for this apparent ambiguity is that the shorter time period is derived from the later accession date and the longer from the earlier one, as the difference between the lengths of time given for the start of rebuilding the Temple is the same as the difference in time between the two accession dates, three years. But I believe a little more is required to justify this assumption before we can safely adopt it here.

In the late first century CE the Judaic population would almost certainly only have recognized Herod's accession *de facto,* as this was the year that the Romans defeated their armies and succeeded in imposing Herod on them. The Romans, on the other hand, would have insisted on the year the Senate declared Herod king of the Jews, his accession *de jure*, as the definitive year. It is the first of these that appears in the earlier of Josephus's books and the second in the later book. It should also be remembered here that Josephus was a turncoat: he began his life as a Jew but ended it as a Roman. This makes it conceivable that when he wrote his earlier book, Josephus was thinking more as a Jew, but by the time he wrote his second he was more romanized. Furthermore, in the preface to *The Jewish Wars* he writes:

> I have proposed to myself, for the sake of such as live under the government of the Romans, to translate those books into the Greek tongue, which I formerly composed in the language of our country, and sent to the Upper Barbarians.

while in *Antiquities of the Jews* he says:

> Now I have undertaken the present work, as thinking it
> will appear to all the Greeks worthy of their study.

In other words he wrote the first book for the Jewish
communities of the Roman Empire, whose families had not
lived in Israel for generations, and the second one for the
non-Jewish, romanized residents of the Empire. This is not
total confirmation for my premise, but it does indicate a shift
in perspective between the two books, in the same direction
as that in his life, and it does not require us to assume that
Josephus made a mistake, something for which there is no
evidence whatsoever.

So in order to find the year in which the temple rebuild
began we need only to follow Josephus's lead. The range of
years for the eighteenth year of Herod's reign *de jure* is given
by the following: ([714 AUC + 17 =] 731 AUC to [715 AUC + 18
=] 733 AUC) **23 to 21 BCE**. (The fifteenth year of Herod's reign
de facto would lead us to the longer year range of 23 to 20
BCE. But this range should not be used because the year-range
for Herod's accession *de facto* was itself calculated by adding
a period of elapsed time to the accession *de jure* and not
derived from the independent evidence, as this proved to be
unreliable.)

If we now apply forty-six elapsed years to the year range
of 22 to 21 BCE we arrive at the years of ([731 AUC + 46 =] 777
AUC to [733 AUC + 46 =] 779 AUC) **24 to 26 CE** for the 'temple
riposte' and first Passover of Jesus' public life.

The third reference we need to examine now is the
Lucan one that relates specifically to the beginning of Jesus'
ministry:

> When Jesus began his work he was about thirty years old.
> (Luke 3: 23)

When we first encountered this reference, in the Nativity
section, I applied this information to the year of the census

of Quirinius, 6 CE+/-1, arriving at the range of year 33 CE to 39 CE. The necessity for the beginning of Jesus' ministry to also occur during the governorship of Pontius Pilate then required us to reduce the range to 33 CE to 36 CE, making him between the ages of 28 and 31 at this time. But consideration of the 'not yet 50 rebuke' suggested he needed to be at least 41 years old in the year 35 CE, which quite clearly he could not have been.

If we now reapply the age range of 30 +/-2 to the range of years we developed from the evidence of Matthew and Josephus for Jesus' birth, we find it yields the following range of years for the beginning of Jesus' ministry: ([742 AUC + 28 =] 770 AUC to [749 AUC + 32 =] 781 AUC) **17 CE to 28 CE**.

It's time for a recap:

The fifteenth year of Tiberius	**27 to 29** CE
'Forty-six years since the Temple rebuild began' riposte	**23 to 26** CE
Jesus about 30 years of age from the census of Quirinius	**34 to 36** CE
Jesus about 30 years of age from Matthew and Josephus	**17 to 28** CE

This looks like a fairly satisfactory result. Notably the range of years for Jesus being about 30, derived from the census taken on the deposition of Archelaus, seems to confirm that we should no longer consider this as the time of Jesus' birth. So if we now focus our attention on the range of years derived from the evidence of Matthew and Josephus, we find it blankets the other two ranges of years, thereby telling us nothing that we did not already know about the time when Jesus began his ministry.

However if we now look only at the other two pieces of evidence, together with the references they support, their date ranges and in the order required by the consensus, we discover that something else is seriously amiss here.

The fifteenth year of Tiberius, the baptism at Bethania and the beginning of Jesus' public life	**27 to 29** CE
The 'forty-six years since the Temple rebuild began' riposte at the first Passover of Jesus' public life	**23 to 26** CE

These two year-ranges indicate that these events occurred in the reverse order to that required by both the Fourth Gospel and the consensus. This order also defies common sense, because the first Passover of Jesus' public life cannot have occurred before the beginning of his public life.

This chronologically insupportable sequence is, I believe, the best kept secret in this field of research. I say this because of the simple fact that every other researcher must have discovered it at some point, and yet not one of them, to my knowledge, has ever either admitted to or demonstrated it. What they have all done is to 'accommodate' it by using one, or more, of the following strategies:

- To pull the year of the First Passover forward in time by assuming Josephus made a mistake when recording the year the temple rebuild began, and adding up to three years to the dates above to create an overlap.
- To push the fifteenth year of Tiberius' reign back in time by claiming that Luke used the year in which Tiberius received his provincial powers (12 or 13 CE) as the starting year for this calculation, in order to create an overlap.
- To blur the distinction between the beginning of Jesus' public life and the beginning of his ministry:
  * by treating these references as if they provided two different ways of deriving a date for a single event
  * by employing the Lucan reference that Jesus was about 30 when he began his work to obfuscate the issue further.
- By silently invoking the strategy that 'near enough is good enough'.

(There may be other strategies, but these are the ones I have encountered.)

I do not believe any of these strategies are viable, and I hope the manner in which I have derived the relevant dates will persuade you that they have hidden the problem, not resolved it. But before I proceed with my own attempt to provide a solution, I must consider the one strategy above that I have not already addressed.

I do have some sympathy with the idea that 'near enough is good enough' with respect to the derivation of the year ranges from the evidence available to us, because there are two opposing forces in play here: the desire to have a single year for every dateable event, and the need to derive a broad enough range of years to accommodate every possible numerically and historically accurate interpretation of the evidence. But it is important to remember that to add another, unnecessary year to a range is just as wrong as reducing a range by unjustified selection. So no, near enough is just not good enough.

Now, if we take the latest possible year for the riposte at the first Passover, 26 CE, and the earliest possible year for the fifteenth year of Tiberius' reign, 27 CE, we could possibly convince ourselves that the difference is of no account, as they are adjacent years. But to do so would be delusional for the following reasons. The year 27 CE is the least likely of the three possible years for the fifteenth year of Tiberius, as it is based on his accession as co-emperor, and the latest possible year for the first Passover is dependent on the three elements of the calculation all being at their furthest extreme; the accession *de jure* of Herod the Great, the eighteenth year of his reign and forty-six years after that. But even if we accept both the extremes of these two ranges, however improbable they are, we are still left with the fact that there is no overlap possible, so the order of events required cannot be supported by the dates.

Nevertheless I still believe there is a truth here that accommodates all of the evidence, without changing the order of the events, without requiring the dates of historical events to be manipulated and without compromising any

of the rules of engagement that I set myself before I began
this investigation. The concept I am about to propose is very
simple, but explaining it is not.

I believe that what follows is:

The Gospel truth

If the Lucan reference is correct, and Jesus began his public
life in the fifteenth year of Tiberius, then the Johannine
reference cannot be correct, and the Passover that occurred
forty-six years after the Temple rebuild began cannot have
been the first Passover of his public life. On the other hand,
if the Passover that was forty-six years since the Temple
rebuild began was the first Passover of his public life, then
the public life of Jesus could not have begun in the fifteenth
year of Tiberius. Therefore either one of these associations is
incorrect, or both of them are.

If neither of these events occurred when the two
Evangelists say they did, then all we have to work with is
Luke's statement that Jesus was 'about 30 years old when he
began his work'. When we explored this, we discovered that
it allowed the ministry to have begun in either of the year
ranges 34 to 36 CE or 17 to 28 CE. However, we have already
excluded the first of these two ranges from consideration, as
it was derived from Jesus being born in the year of the census
taken on the deposition of Archelaus, which we now believe
is insupportable. This leaves us with only the somewhat
unsatisfactory, and all-embracing, range of the twelve years,
from 17 to 28 CE for the beginning of Jesus' ministry.

So in what other way can we approach this conundrum in
order to resolve it? Perhaps by taking:

A different perspective

It was the bizarre, and frankly impossible, sequence of events
in Luke's account that led me to what I believe is the solution
to the problem. In order to understand the sequence I found

it was necessary to try to look at the situation from Luke's point of view.

Unlike the other three Evangelists, Luke had no first-hand knowledge of these events. He came into the picture after Jesus' execution, as a disciple of Paul of Tarsus, and in this capacity he went to Jerusalem with Paul, just before his trial, where he met Simon Peter and James, Jesus' brother. We have no idea whether he had conversations with these two worthies, but even if he didn't, there is a strong chance that he did get to speak to other, less exalted followers who had had some contact with Jesus and/or the other Apostles. From them he may have acquired those little extra pieces of information that appear in his Gospel.

He admits in his introduction that he researched his subject in order to produce a 'connected narrative', and we know that, unlike the other Evangelists, he deliberately set out to place Jesus' life in the historical timeline. When he began his research we know that he had access to either the Q-document, or one or both of the other Synoptic Gospels. So from them he would have learned the following sequence of events:

- John emerged from the wilderness and began to baptise people in the River Jordan.
- Jesus began his public life when he arrived at where John was and was baptised by him before the dove descended upon him.
- Jesus then went into the wilderness where he suffered temptation.
- When he emerged from the wilderness he found that John had been arrested.
- Jesus began to proclaim the Gospel of God, thereby beginning his ministry.

Why then did he change that sequence to this?

- John emerged from the wilderness and began to baptise people in the River Jordan.

- John was arrested.
- Jesus arrived at where John was and where he was baptised by him before the 'dove' descended upon him.
- Luke tells us that Jesus was about 30 when he began his work.
- Jesus then went into the wilderness, where he suffered temptation.
- When he emerged from the wilderness Jesus began to proclaim the Gospel of God, thereby demonstrating the beginning of his ministry.

I believe that Luke accomplished several things by this order. First, he disconnected the arrest of John from the beginning of Jesus' ministry, thereby removing or reducing the possibility of cause and effect that may be inferred from the accounts of both Mark and Matthew. Second, by announcing that Jesus began his work 'when he was about 30', immediately after Jesus' baptism by John and the 'dove incident', he implied a different and preferable causality. By doing this he also combined the beginning of Jesus' public life with the beginning of his ministry by placing both immediately after the 'dove incident'.

But he also accomplished something else when he did this. By embedding John's arrest between two references to the one baptism of which he knew, the one that our knowledge of the Fourth Gospel allows us to identify as the first baptism, at Bethania, he implied that John was arrested there. But we know this is not so because the Fourth Gospel also tells us that John was arrested at or just after the baptism at Aenon.

From this it is but a small step to the realization that by placing John's arrest at Bethania, Luke also drew this baptism forward in time, in his own chronological order. From this Luke would then have believed that if he could find a date for one of these two events he would also have the date of the other. I suggest that only one of these two events was likely to have yielded to research in the Roman Empire during the latter part of the first century CE: John's arrest. Logic dictates, I believe, that the arrest of a holy man by a king is much more likely to have been a matter of record than the emergence of that holy man from the wilderness in order to perform baptisms.

In other words, the 'fifteenth year of Tiberius' was the year of John's arrest and not the year that he emerged from the wilderness to baptise sinners. If you think this is fanciful, then look again at the accounts given by Mark and Matthew, and imagine if you can that you are seeing this for the first time. Then ask yourself this question: what length of time would you have imagined for the period between John's emergence and his arrest if the Fourth Gospel did not exist? I'm guessing you would answer something like 'forty days plus a few weeks; months at the most'. I believe that is exactly the answer Luke would have given.

From the above reasoning I believe that John the Baptist was arrested in the '15th year of Tiberius', from **780/27 to 782/29,** and that Luke incorrectly deduced that this was also the year that John had begun *his* work at Bethania. Hence he also assumed that the public life of Jesus began in the same year.

You may find my explanation for the bizarre order of events in Luke's Gospel speculative or even fanciful. There is, after all, no way we can be certain that it is correct. But does that change anything? I believe not, because the reasoning that I have used to achieve the above result is not actually dependent upon it.

A theory requires proof, and in this instance it can only come from its application:

22 to 26 CE	John the Baptist begins his ministry, and identifies Jesus at the 'dove incident'. Jesus then begins his public life, at Bethania, either late in the year before, or early in the same year as ...
23 to 26 CE	Jesus goes to Jerusalem for the first Passover, where he evicts the traders from the Temple and receives the 'forty-six years riposte'.
26 to 29 CE	Jesus and John go to baptise people at Aenon, which may have occurred either late in the year before, or in the same year as ...

27 to 29 CE   John the Baptist is arrested at, or shortly
               after, his visit to Aenon, in the fifteenth
               year of the reign of Tiberius and during the
               governorship of Pontius Pilate.

We now have a chronology that is not impossible and, perhaps
surprisingly, *does not change the order of any of the key events
required by either the Gospels (except Luke's) or the consensus.* Its
major difference, apart from the fact that it is chronologically
possible, is that it could lengthen considerably the time
between the beginning of John's ministry and his arrest, and
hence between Bethania and Aenon. The gap is between
about nine months and seven years, and the shortest period
this allows is still identical to that usually required by the
consensus, as you can see above.

Again, if you doubt the validity of my proposal, ask yourself
this question: if only the Gospels of Luke and John existed,
what then would the consensus look like? I suggest it would
be identical to the list above.

Unfortunately we are still none the wiser with respect to the
time and place of the actual beginning of Jesus' ministry. This
is unavoidable, because the evidence of the Four Evangelists
is inconclusive and contradictory. All we can say for sure is
that it was at some time between the years **22 and 29** CE: from
just after the 'dove incident' until just after John's arrest at
Aenon.

Loose ends

You will have noticed that I have omitted two other significant
events from the new chronology: the baptism of Jesus by
John, and the temptation in the wilderness. We are also in a
position now that requires us to ask the following question.
If the length of time between Bethania and Aenon is likely to
be up to six years longer than was previously assumed, what
was Jesus doing during that period? There is also another
problem which is far from insignificant, and cannot be

ignored. I shall call it the 'aberrant incident'. These issues we shall now look at in this final part of our investigation 'of the beginnings'.

The baptism of Jesus

I have omitted this from the chronology not because we do not know when it occurred, but because we do not know *whether* it occurred. There are two possible sources of evidence that it did occur, the Q-document and/or the lead Synoptic Gospel. That it did not occur is implied by the Fourth Gospel. Its author was the only one of the Evangelists to have been at Bethania at the time, and yet he makes no mention of the baptism. It is true, as I have been at pains to explain earlier, that a lack of evidence for an event is not proof that it did not occur, but if it did occur and the author of the Fourth Gospel did not record it he must have had a very good reason (which can only be guessed at). Fortunately however, this does not affect the chronology in any way at all.

The temptation in the wilderness

My omission of the temptation in the wilderness is on two grounds. First, we do not know when it happened, and second, we do not know *whether* it happened. If it did occur, then rather like the beginning of the ministry itself, it could have begun at any time from just after the 'dove incident' at Bethania to just before the arrest of John. But again, the Fourth Gospel does not record it, and does not seem to leave room for it at either of the times suggested by the Synoptists. However, it does allow for the possibility that it occurred at a particular time, and it also allows for an entirely different explanation.

The 'different explanation' is simply this. The writer of the Q-document, if it existed, or the author of the first of the Synoptic Gospels, if it did not, might have suspected, or even known, that there was a gap in his knowledge of the time between Bethania and John's arrest. Knowing nothing of what took place, or how long this period lasted, he might then have used the idea of the temptation in the wilderness as a metaphor for all that he did not know (but that the author of the Fourth Gospel did know). In other words the temptation could be a way of representing all of the extra material that resides only within the Fourth Gospel. This is pure speculation on my part, and it has no bearing on the chronology; but it is, I think, worth considering as a possible way of explaining the differences in the accounts.

On the other hand if the temptation was an actual event, which is not recorded in the Fourth Gospel, we have to ask ourselves where, and hence when, it could have been placed in the sequence of events in this Gospel. The Synoptists allow it to have occurred anywhere between Bethania and Aenon, but before the arrest of John. But although the Fourth Gospel theoretically allows the temptation to have been at any time in this period, the narrative is not so generous, and in fact only suggests one location. After the first Passover of Jesus' public life and the slightly clandestine meeting of Jesus and Nicodemus, at night, we have the following:

> After this Jesus went into Judaea with his disciples, stayed there with them and baptised ... at Aenon, near Salim ... this was before John's imprisonment..
>
> (John 3: 22–24)

The statement that 'Jesus went into Judaea' implies that before doing so he was somewhere other than Judaea, and yet the first Passover and the meeting with Nicodemus took place in Jerusalem, which is in Judaea. Perhaps it was the conversation with Nicodemus or the reaction he received when he overturned the traders' tables in the Temple that led Jesus into the wilderness. But the wilderness is also in Judaea. So there is an implication that Jesus was somewhere else, doing something else, for at least part of this time: in

Galilee, perhaps? This leads us to the consideration of the final 'loose end'.

The missing years

Although we do not know exactly how much time elapsed between the events at Bethania and Aenon, it is difficult to imagine that there is a long period here for which there is absolutely no trace of Jesus' whereabouts. The most likely explanation is that we do know at least some of what Jesus was doing at this time, but that the events were recorded in the wrong places. It is already suspected by many researchers that some events that appear in the Synoptics are out of sequence. Is it possible to identify any of them that might be more at home in this gap? I believe it is. The best candidates can be characterized by the following: they took place in Galilee, they appear in the Synoptics, and they do not appear in the Fourth Gospel. I suggest the last of these conditions because the author of the Fourth Gospel seems to have spent more time with Jesus in Judaea than he did in Galilee. To me, there is one very obvious candidate:

> Jesus was waiting by the Sea of Galilee when he saw Simon and his brother Andrew on the lake at work with a casting net: for they were fishermen. Jesus said to them, 'Come with me and I will make you fishers of men.' And at once they left their nets and followed him. When he had gone a little farther he saw James son of Zebedee and his brother John ... he called them; and leaving their father ... they went off and followed him.
>
> (Mark 1: 16–20: see also Matthew 4: 18–22, Luke 5: 1–11)

In Mark's account this is Jesus' first meeting with the two pairs of brothers. Yet they immediately, and without further ado, leave their jobs, families and homes to follow him. The Fourth Gospel in contrast tells us that Jesus had already met, and recruited, Simon Peter and Andrew, as well as the unnamed disciple, Philip and Nathaneal, at Bethania, where they were witnesses to the Baptist's identification of Jesus as 'God's Chosen One'. After this some, or all, of them may have gone with him to Cana for the wedding, on to Capharnaum, to Jerusalem for the first Passover and then on to Aenon.

Of the four disciples gathered up by the sea of Galilee, according to all of the Synoptists, James and John Boanerges were absent from Bethania, according to the Fourth Gospel. It seems reasonable to assume here that they were recruited at some time during the return to Galilee from Bethania and before the group's arrival at Aenon, where John the Baptist was arrested. It also seems credible that after the first Passover, Simon Peter and Andrew returned to their homes to tell their families and friends that they were going to be disciples of Jesus and might be gone for some time. Then presumably Jesus went to their locality to collect them after the first Passover, and just before going to Aenon for the baptism, which seems more probable.

As I have said before, this is proof of nothing. But, it does, I believe, provide a better explanation for these men's behaviour than those implied in the Synoptics.

The aberrant incident

As you have seen in this section, a central event which all researchers use when attempting to derive a year for the beginning of Jesus' ministry is that known as the first Passover of his public life. However I have not seen it acknowledged that there is a problem with doing this, and not an insignificant one. To understand the problem let us first return to the full text, as shown in the Fourth Gospel.

> As it was near the time of the Jewish Passover, *Jesus went up to Jerusalem. There he found in the temple the dealers in cattle, sheep and pigeons, and the money-changers seated at their tables. Jesus made a whip of cords and drove them out of the*

temple, sheep, cattle, and all. He upset the tables of the money-changers scattering their coins. Then he turned on the dealers in pigeons: 'Take them out,' he said; 'you must not turn my Father's house into a market.' His disciples recalled the words of Scripture, 'Zeal for thy house will destroy me.' The Jews challenged Jesus: 'What sign', they asked, 'can you show as authority for your action?' **'Destroy the temple,' Jesus replied, 'and in three days I will raise it again.' They said, 'It has taken forty-six years to build this temple. Are you going to raise it again in three days?'**

(John 2:13–21)

The section highlighted in bold is the part used to date the first Passover. The section in italic is the part that causes the problem. That is because this incident bears a close resemblance to one described by Mark (11: 15–19), Luke (19: 45–48) and Matthew (21: 12–13). These three Evangelists all place these events either during or just after Palm Sunday, a matter of only days before Good Friday, and immediately before the *last* Passover of Jesus' life. Let me quote the passages in full to clarify this:

So they came to Jerusalem, and he went into the temple and began driving out those who bought and sold in the temple. He upset the tables of the money-changers and the seats of the dealers in pigeons; and he would not allow anyone to use the temple courtyards as a thoroughfare for carrying goods. Then he began to teach them, and said, 'Does not scripture say, "My house shall be a house of prayer for all the nations"? But you have made it a robbers' cave.'

(Mark 11: 15–17)

Then he went into the temple and began driving out the traders, with these words: 'Scripture says, "My house shall be a house of prayer"; but you have made it a robbers' cave.'

(Luke 19: 45–46)

> Jesus then went into the temple and drove out all who
> were buying and selling in the temple precincts; he upset
> the tables of the money-changers and the seats of the
> dealers in pigeons; and said to them 'My house shall be
> called a house of prayer; but you are making it a robbers'
> cave.'
>
> (Matthew 21: 12–13)

The similarities between the passages in Mark, Luke and
Matthew are clear. Their accounts are also similar enough to
the account in the Fourth Gospel to make it seem likely that
they refer to the same event. However, all other researchers
that I have encountered follow the consensus in regarding the
incident described in the Synoptic Gospels and the one in the
Fourth Gospel as two separate events.

The *New Advent Catholic Encyclopaedia*[31] has this to say on
the subject:

> The purification of the Temple is referred by John to the
> beginning of the Saviour's ministry, while the Synoptists
> narrate it at the close. But it is by no means proven that
> this purification occurred but once. The critics bring
> forward not a single objective reason why we should not
> hold that the incident, under the circumstances related
> in the Synoptics, as well as those of the Fourth Gospel,
> had its historical place at the beginning and at the end of
> the public life of Jesus.

I beg to differ for not one, but three objective reasons:

- None of the Gospels record two events of this nature.
- The writer of the original document that became the
  Fourth Gospel was the 'disciple he loved', an eye-witness
  to the events of the final week, and to Jesus' Passion. How
  could he have failed to either notice or record the second
  purge of the Temple, if it had occurred?

---

31 *NACE*: Gospel of St. John: Historical Genuineness (1).

- If we take the event exactly as described in the Fourth Gospel (including the part highlighted in bold) and move it to where the Synoptics place their accounts, it would present us with an improbable narrative or an impossible chronology, or both.

I believe that once again we have here an event that the author of either the Q-document or the original Synoptic Gospel knew of. But crucially, he did not know either the time span or the events between the baptism at Bethania and the arrest of John, so he could not place it correctly. Instead he positioned it where, and hence when, he thought it made most sense. The other Synoptists followed his lead, providing us with further evidence that the account given by the author of the Fourth Gospel is sequentially more accurate than those of the Synoptics.

From this I maintain that the temple purge recorded in the Fourth Gospel, and placed at the time of the First Passover of Jesus' public life, along with the 'forty-six years riposte', is correctly positioned in the sequence of events, whilst that recorded in all of the Synoptics has been incorrectly placed in the final week of Jesus' life.

Summary

Both the beginning of Jesus' public life and the beginning of his ministry have proved to be troublesome to locate in the timeline of history. However, I believe that by allowing the evidence to guide us we have discovered an alternative way to interpret the evidence that does not require the use of unlikely selections for the dates of associated historical events. Remarkably, this has not changed the order of any of the key events of Jesus' life between the emergence from the wilderness of John the Baptist and his arrest.

It is true that we have not yet been able to locate the actual moment when Jesus' ministry began through direct evidence. There are good reasons for this failure. The Fourth Gospel, although it provides a more or less continuous narrative through all of these events, is silent about this beginning, while Matthew and Mark place it after John's arrest. Luke, on the other hand, seems to place it at Bethania, while indicating that it occurred after the temptation in the wilderness. But does this not demonstrate the reality of the situation? Different people would have had different opinions about when that moment was. Their conclusions would have depended on how, when and where they first encountered Jesus, and how much they knew about him before that moment.

We must not forget, though, that this investigation is about placing Jesus' life in the historical timeline, using every piece of evidence provided by the Gospels. One purpose of doing so is to confirm that Jesus' existence as recorded in the Gospels is consistent with the historical record.

This is what we have discovered directly from the evidence:

23 to 26 CE   46 years since Temple rebuild began: the first Passover.

27 to 29 CE   15th year of Tiberius's reign: John the Baptist arrested.

We can now move on to the most significant event in the life of Jesus.

Stained glass from the church of St Peter, Ringland, Norfolk

The year of his crucifixion

To walk in the steps of the consensus here and chronicle the remainder of Jesus' life, from Aenon to Golgotha, will not help us to arrive at a year for his crucifixion. The Synoptics contain no further chronological evidence to guide us, and it is almost exclusively the evidence found in the Fourth Gospel that is used by researchers. But even there we find no new clues for the period between John's arrest and the crucifixion of Jesus. The execution of John would have been such a milestone, but even though Josephus mentions this event, neither he nor any other remaining source provides a way of divining its date.

So where do we start? All we have at the moment are two dates to work between:

27 to 29 CE   The year that John the Baptist was arrested at Aenon.

36 CE   The year that Pilate was recalled to Rome, and hence the latest year for the last Passover and the crucifixion of Jesus.

From this all that we can ascertain is that the *earliest possible* year for the crucifixion of Jesus is 27 CE while the *latest possible* year is 36 CE.

We can improve on this a little, as there are recurring festivals recorded in the Fourth Gospel between these events. But we cannot use this information to locate the last year of Jesus' life exactly, because we do not know whether the author of the Fourth Gospel recorded every year's festivals over this time period. Therefore all we can expect to achieve from this exercise is a later *earliest possible* year.

Only one Passover is recorded in the Fourth Gospel between John's arrest and the last Passover of Jesus' life. It is mentioned while Jesus was in Galilee, just before the feeding of the 5,000.

> It was near the time of Passover, the great Jewish festival.
> (John 6: 4)

Although we are not taken to this Passover by the Fourth Gospel and neither is it mentioned again, we can nevertheless be certain that this Passover was not the last of Jesus' life. This is because after the feeding of the 5,000 we are taken to two other festivals, a Feast of Tabernacles (John 7: 2) and a Feast of Dedication (John 10: 22). Tabernacles is held in the autumn, after the harvest, and the Feast of Dedication is held in December. The first mention of the last Passover does not occur until John 11: 55. So we can be certain that the Passover alluded to at John 6: 4 was additional to the last one, and it could have been the Passover of any of the years from 27 to 35 CE.

But that is all the help we get. Many scholars believe that an unnamed festival referred to in the Fourth Gospel (John 5: 1) was also a Passover. However just as many believe just as fervently that it was not, so it would be dubious to use it in an effort to improve on the *earliest possible* date for the Crucifixion. Therefore, we can now only adjust the *earliest possible* year for the crucifixion to 28 CE.

In my introduction[32] I told a cautionary tale regarding the use of the 'patristic testimonies' as evidence in this investigation. The comments there about the questionable reliability of this information still hold, but let us take a look at what they have to offer on the subject of the date of Jesus' execution. I shall do so not least because ignoring their evidence could be regarded as avoidance of difficult material and an attempt by me to 'manage' the available evidence.

---

32 Preparing the Way : Other sources, p. 14.

Of Patrizi and the patristic testimonies

Francis Xavier Patrizi was born in 1797 CE and entered the Society of Jesus in 1814 CE. He was ordained as a priest in 1824 CE, and later became professor of Sacred Scripture and Hebrew at the Roman College. He was a prolific writer, with twenty-one books to his credit, all of them biblical and ascetic in nature. *De Evangeliis* was published in 1853 CE and is, according to the *New Advent Catholic Encyclopaedia*, the work in which he gathered together the 'patristic testimonies' he had researched. I have been unable to obtain Patrizi's work, but a number of more recent publications outline and discuss his findings. However, none of these secondary works give a clear provenance for Patrizi's sources.

Patrizi evidently claimed that Jesus died in either the fifteenth or sixteenth year of Tiberius, during the consulship of the Gemini (the twins) Fufius and Rubellius, forty-two years before the destruction of Jerusalem, and twelve years before the conversion of the centurion Cornelius. We must bear in mind that circular reasoning might have been involved in calculating some, or even all, of these dates, so we shall proceed with caution.

According to the Consular List the Geminis were consuls in 29 CE. By my reckoning the fifteenth and sixteenth years of Tiberius fell between 27 and 30 CE, although the year 29 CE is the most likely, as it was the sixteenth year of his joint reign with Augustus and the fifteenth year of his absolute reign.

Forty-two years before the fall of Jerusalem also takes us to the possible years of 28 or 29 CE. It should be appreciated though that this claim could not have been made until *after* Jerusalem fell in 70 CE.

The conversion of the centurion Cornelius is documented in the Acts of the Apostles, and marks the beginning of the preaching of the Gospel to the Gentiles. It is not possible to derive the year of Cornelius's conversion from the information provided by Luke, nor is it possible to derive an accurate interval between the crucifixion and this event.

But, even if we knew Patrizi's source for the interval we would still be unable to calculate the year of the crucifixion without knowing the year of Cornelius' conversion. There is therefore no basis for Patrizi's claim that Jesus was executed twelve years before this event.

Nevertheless, the 'patristic testimonies' used here all seem to focus on the three years from 28 to 30 CE for the execution of Jesus. We have already discovered that it must have occurred between 28 CE and 36 CE, but this does not mean that the overlap between Patrizi's range and ours gives the solution to the problem because, without having sight of his sources, we cannot safely conclude that they are valid.

But I believe there is another way that we can do this, by using two pieces of evidence from two different Gospels, in concert, and in a way I have never seen used elsewhere.

Of Luke and the Fourth Gospel

There are two references in the Gospels that we have already encountered that, if used together, might provide the best opportunity to discover the actual year of Jesus' crucifixion. The first comes from the Fourth Gospel, and implies that Jesus was in his forties at the time of the 'not yet fifty rebuke'. The second is provided by Luke, who tells us that Jesus was 'about thirty when he began his work'. I believe it is possible to use these two independent, though temporally linked, fragments of evidence to narrow the range of possible years for the crucifixion. Table 3 shows what I mean.

The 'master row' in this matrix is row 2 (starting 23 CE), as it represents the *earliest possible year* for the beginning of Jesus' ministry, and the full range of possible ages we have for this event, from Luke's 'about 30' reference. From this we can then work forwards until we reach the *latest possible year* allowable for the crucifixion, adding Jesus' age for each possible year. The first set of shaded cells down column 1 (23 to 29 CE) represent the full range of years permissible for the ministry to have begun, and the shaded cells to the right of these are those that

Table 3

Year of birth	10 BCE	9 BCE	8 BCE	7 BCE	6 BCE
23 CE	32	31	30	29	28
24 CE	33	32	31	30	29
25 CE	34	33	32	31	30
26 CE	35	34	33	32	31
27 CE	36	34	34	33	32
28 CE	37	36	35	34	33
29 CE	38	37	36	35	34
30 CE	39	38	37	36	35
31 CE	40	39	38	37	36
32 CE	41	40	39	38	37
33 CE	42	41	40	39	38
34 CE	43	42	41	40	39
35 CE	44	43	42	41	40
36 CE	45	44	43	42	41

also allow for Jesus to have been 'about 30' at the time. The lower range of shaded cells in columns 2 to 5 show ages that conform with the 'not yet 50' rebuke, and the lower range of shaded cells indicate the range of years possible for the year of his crucifixion. The years highlighted in bold are the possible years for the fifteenth year of Tiberius' reign. Lastly, the first row of the matrix shows the year of birth required to support the ages in each column.

From this we can clearly see that by combining these two pieces of evidence we have not only reduced the number of years possible for Jesus' execution, to the four years of **33 to 36** CE, we have also reduced the number of years for the beginning of his ministry to **23 to 26** CE, and those for his birth to **10 to 7** BCE. We have also, incidentally, shown that all of the years provided by the 'patristic testimonies' are excluded by this exercise.

If these results are correct, which I believe they are, then the last Passover, trial and crucifixion of Jesus occurred several years later than is commonly believed by exegetes.

Of course, others might have come to the same conclusion, but by different reasoning. I think the views of two other commentators deserve some consideration here, not least because if I did not consider their claims, it might suggest that I am either unaware of their existence or unwilling to consider their evidence.

Of Loisy and Suetonius

Alfred Firmin Loisy[33] wrote in *The Gospel and the Church* (1902) that:

> The author of [the Gospel of] John's use of allegory to describe Jesus' body as Herod's Temple, which according to Jesus' Jewish opponents, required 46 years to build, was meant as a symbolic comment on Jesus' age at the time of his ministry. If accurate, such comments would place the death of Jesus in the reign of the Roman Emperor Claudius (41–54 CE).

The passage in the Fourth Gospel to which Loisy refers here is contained within the verses that chronicle the events

---

33 Alfred Firmin Loisy (28 February 1857–1 June 1940) was a French Roman Catholic priest, professor and theologian who became the intellectual standard bearer for Biblical Modernism in the Roman Catholic Church. He was a critic of traditional views of the biblical creation myth, and argued that biblical criticism could be applied to interpreting scripture. His theological positions brought him into conflict with the leading Catholics of his era, including Pope Leo XIII and Pope Pius X. In 1893,he was dismissed as a professor from the Institut Catholique de Paris. His books were condemned by the Vatican, and in 1908 he was excommunicated. (Source: Wikipedia.)

that occurred at the First Passover of Jesus' public life (John 2: 13–22). The first eight of these verses begin with Jesus purging the temple, an event I have referred to as the 'aberrant incident'. This is followed by his reference to the temple as his father's house. These incidents together provoked the following exchange:

> The Jews challenged Jesus: 'What sign', they asked, 'can you show as authority for your action?' 'Destroy this temple,' Jesus replied, 'and in three days I will raise it again.' They said 'It has taken 46 years to build this temple. Are you going to raise it again in three days?'
>
> (John 2: 19–20)

From these words Loisy deduced the following:

- that the statement made by the Jews claiming the Temple had been under construction for forty-six years 'was meant as a symbolic comment on Jesus' age at the time of his ministry'
- that, 'If accurate, such comments would place the death of Jesus in the reign of the Roman Emperor Claudius.'

It is the next verse from the Fourth Gospel that is the direct basis for the first deduction and therefore, by Loisy's reasoning, the indirect basis for the second:

> But the temple he was speaking of was his body.
>
> (John 2: 21)

From this Loisy reasoned that the allegory employed by 'the author of [the Gospel of] John' implies that the '46 years to build the temple' referred to the length of Jesus' life, at that time. But is this statement correct? Doesn't the allegory used here belong to Jesus, and not to the author of the Fourth Gospel? And isn't the use of the allegory used by Jesus here adequately explained by the author of the Gospel in the next verse when he writes that:

> After his resurrection his disciples recalled what he had
> said, and they believed the Scripture and the words that
> Jesus had spoken.
>
> (John 2: 22)

From this I deduce that the man who wrote the Gospel is saying
that Jesus' allegory was predicting his own 'destruction', his
execution, and his subsequent 'rebuilding', his resurrection,
on the third day! The fact that the words of the challenge,
that it had taken '46 years to build' the temple, were uttered
'by the Jews' confirms that they were not a part of the allegory,
merely the inspiration for it. This strategy became a feature of
many of the conversations between Jesus and his opponents
in rhetoric, that he would reply to their loaded questions by
reinterpreting them and using his answer to say something
completely different.

Incidentally, that Jesus' allegory also implies a prediction
does not require us to believe in prophecy. It only requires
us to believe that Jesus and the author of the Fourth Gospel
did so.

If I am correct this would make Loisy's deductions both
incorrect and irrelevant, and we would be justified in
dismissing them without further ado, if it wasn't for the fact
that there is another piece of independent evidence, to which
Loisy does not refer, that nevertheless suggests the possibility
that Jesus was still alive during the reign of Claudius. The
Roman historian known as Suetonius recorded in his *Lives
of the Twelve Caesars* (121 CE) that Claudius expelled the
Jews from Rome for 'making constant disturbances at the
instigation of Chrestus'.[34] Perhaps this was the true source of
Loisy's second 'deduction'.

During this investigation I have not written of Jesus' 'death'

---

34 Gaius Suetonius Tranquillus, commonly known as Suetonius (c.
69–122 CE), was a Roman historian belonging to the equestrian
order who wrote during the early Imperial era of the Roman
Empire. (Source: Wikipedia.)

until this chapter. I have written only of his crucifixion or his execution, because Jesus' 'death' means different things to different people. There are those who believe he simply died on the cross. Others believe that he died on the cross, was brought back to life and later ascended to heaven. Some may regard the ascension as a kind of death, as to them, it was then that he gave up his corporeal existence. Yet others believe that he did not die on the cross at all: either he died a little later, from his wounds, or he survived his wounds and lived for many more years, eventually dying a more natural death.

The limiting factors here are given by the governorship of Pontius Pilate (26 to 36 CE) and the reign of the Emperor Claudius (41 to 54 CE), and there are several interpretations of the above scenarios that allow for Jesus' crucifixion to have taken place during the former interval and for his death to have occurred during the latter interval. So neither the 'deductions' of Loisy nor the evidence of Suetonius *require* Jesus to have been alive at the time of Claudius.

But there is also a far more prosaic explanation possible here, that those 'making constant disturbances at the instigation of Chrestus' were simply Christian protesters evangelizing in the name of their Saviour, even though he was deceased. The death of the leader of a cause has not always resulted in the death of the cause. Indeed the continued existence of Christianity is 'living' proof of this to this very day.

Schonfield's hypothesis

In his ground-breaking book of 1965, *The Passover Plot*, Hugh Schonfield proposed a hypothesis that places the crucifixion of Jesus in the last years of Pilate's governorship of Judaea, 33 CE to 36 CE. The hypothesis is in two parts.

First, Schonfield suggested that there might have been another of the hated Roman censuses in 34 CE (or 35 CE)[35] and

---

35 Here Schonfield has used the two years commonly given for the

that Jesus had been inciting opposition to this in the Temple, leading Pilate to want him eliminated. Although there is no direct evidence of another census at this time, there may well have been one if, as Schonfield reasoned, the census of 6 CE+/-1 in Judaea corresponded with one of a series in Egypt that had a frequency of fourteen years. If this was the case it could well have led to disturbances in Jerusalem at the time of the Passover of 6 CE +/-1 + (2 × 14) = 33 CE to 35 CE. However, the disturbance that Schonfield refers to is the eviction of the traders from the precincts of the Temple during the last week of Jesus' life. This is the 'aberrant incident' that I referred to earlier (see page 94). If I am correct that it should actually be placed at the first Passover of Jesus' public life, this would preclude it from being either related to the census proposed by Schonfield or an immediate cause of Jesus' arrest and execution.

However, it would be unwise to dismiss Schonfield yet, for one very good reason. Subtracting fourteen years from 6 CE +/-1 takes us back to 10 to 8 BCE for Jesus' birth, which overlaps the range of years we found earlier, 12 to 7 BCE, to be possible years for an earlier census and for the nativity.

The second part is more complicated. As we have seen earlier, when Herod the Great died his kingdom was divided between three of his remaining sons, Archelaus, Antipas and Philip. Archelaus became ethnarc of Judaea and Samaria, while his younger full brother Antipas became tetrarch of Galilee and Peraea, and their half-brother Philip became ethnarc of Gaulanitis, Batanaea, Trachonitis and Auranitis. After Archelaus was deposed in 6 CE he was replaced by a Roman governor.

Antipas married Phasaelis, the daughter of King Aretas IV of Nabatea, in what was possibly a diplomatic marriage to aid relations with his troublesome eastern neighbour. But he

census of Quirinius, 6 CE and 7 CE, as the starting point for his calculation, but as I have already shown that there is reason to allow the three years of 6 CE +/-1 for this, I shall use these in my calculations.

later began a relationship with Philip's wife Herodias, which ended his marriage to Phasaelis and resulted in his marrying Herodias,[36] who was a cousin to both Philip and Antipas. Philip died either late in 33 or early in 34 CE. A year later, in the winter of 35–36 CE, King Aretas of Nabatene and Tetrarch Antipas went to war with each other. Antipas lost.

Schonfield reasoned that Antipas and Herodias could not have married until after Philip had died, and from this that John the Baptist would not have been arrested until after the marriage, probably in 34 CE. He then reasoned that John was probably executed on the eve of the Nabatean war, and that this was a factor in, or even the main cause for, that war. He went on to conclude that it is the imprisonment and execution of John the Baptist that governs the date of the ministry and the crucifixion of Jesus, and hence by knowing the time of the former we also know the time of the latter. From this he argued that Jesus was crucified at the Passover of 36 CE.

There are, I believe, some problems with the second part of this hypothesis. First, is Schonfield's claim that Antipas could not have married Herodias until after Philip's death correct? According to Mark:

> Herod (Antipas) had sent and arrested John and put him in prison on account of his brother Philip's wife, Herodias, whom he had married.
>
> (Mark 6: 17)

and again:

> John had told Herod [Antipas] 'You have no right to your brother's wife.'
>
> (Mark 6: 18)

---

36 Some scholars argue that it was Salome, not Herodias, who was Philip's wife, and that the Evangelists made a mistake. I am not convinced by the reasoning I have seen, but it does not affect the outcome of events so I shall continue with the Gospel nomination. (See Wikipedia on 'Philip the Tetrarch'.)

Luke also says:

> But Prince Herod, when he was rebuked by him [John]
> over the affair of his brother's wife Herodias and for his
> other misdeeds, crowned them all by shutting John up
> in prison.
>
> (Luke 3: 19–20)

It is clear here that Antipas had married Herodias before
John's arrest. Furthermore, each of these passages suggest
that Philip was still alive at the time of John's arrest. If Philip
had already died, Mark and Luke would surely have referred
to Herodias as his widow, not as his wife. Was this not the
basis of John's objections and opposition: that the marriage
of Antipas and Herodias was bigamous and hence unlawful?

Second, I take issue with the assertions that the
imprisonment and execution of John the Baptist governed
the date of the ministry and the crucifixion of Jesus. There is
no actual evidence that requires the arrest of John the Baptist
to have been related to, or a causal factor for, the beginning
of Jesus' ministry, although the fact that the latter closely
followed the former, in the Gospels of Mark and Matthew,
does allow for the possibility that they could have been causally
connected. But there is nothing in the Gospels, or the second
part of Schonfield's hypothesis, that requires Jesus' execution
to have been related to or dependant on that of John. This,
I feel, is a simple example of the logical fallacy of *post hoc
ergo propter hoc*. In addition have already discovered that the
Baptist's arrest was most likely to have taken place in 'the
fifteenth year of Tiberius' reign' (27 to 29 CE) which would
render his suggestion that this event was related directly to
the death of Philip, in 33 or 34 CE, untenable.

There is also no evidence to require the causal connection
between John's death and the Nabatean war that Schonfield
suspects, and I would suggest the most likely reason for King
Aretas' aggression was the treatment of his daughter by
Antipas.

If there was a census carried out at this time, Schonfield's hypothesis also requires a second purge of the Temple, and one at which the Temple riposte would not have featured, just as suggested by the Synoptists and the Consensus. In 'The aberrant incident' (see page 94) I argued that this was extremely unlikely, as it had not been recorded in the Fourth Gospel, the author of which had been a witness to the events of the last week of Jesus' life. But this does not preclude the possibility of there having been a second purge of the temple at an earlier Passover, one that the Fourth Evangelist had not attended, and possibly in the year of Schonfield's suggested census of 33 to 35 CE.

There is just such a possibility, one that we encountered briefly, earlier, and it resides within the Fourth Gospel.

> Some time later Jesus withdrew to the farthest shore of the Sea of Galilee...It was near the time of the Passover...
> (John 6: 1–4)

This passage introduces the incident known as the 'feeding of the 5,000'. The narrative continues through this event to the 'walking on water', to the 'food of eternal life', to 'Jesus the bread of life', to 'a challenge to the disciples' faith', and to 'a challenge from Jesus' brothers', without taking us to this Passover at Jerusalem. We know this because the last of these episodes begins:

> Afterwards Jesus went into Galilee. He wished to avoid Judaea because the Jews were looking for a chance to kill him ... the Jewish Feast of Tabernacles was close at hand ...
> (John 7: 1–3)

As the Feast of Tabernacles is an autumnal feast to celebrate the harvest, we know that the Passover mentioned previously had passed without the author of the Fourth Gospel recording it. We do not know the reason for this, although as I have said before, I have come to the belief that the Fourth Evangelist only recorded what he witnessed. (This does not mean that he recorded everything he witnessed.) This allows the possibility that a second purging of the temple could have occurred at this Passover, if it occurred at all, and this could imply that this was also the year of Schonfield's hypothetical second census in 33 to 35 CE. It is also intriguing that the above reference also mentions that 'the Jews were looking for a chance to kill him [Jesus]' after this Passover.

Between this Feast of Tabernacles and the last Passover of Jesus' life there is only one more festival mentioned, again in the Fourth Gospel: the December Feast of Dedication (John 10: 22). So it is possible that all of these events occurred in the year before that of the crucifixion, also placing this event in one of the years 33 to 35 CE. We have already seen from our investigation that, by combining Luke's 'about 30 when he began his work' reference (3: 23) with the 'not yet 50 rebuke' (John 8: 57) made just after the above Feast of Tabernacles, Jesus must have been executed in the years 33 to 36 CE, making my slightly modified version of Schonfield's hypothesis a serious candidate for inclusion in this chronology. The only drawback is that there is absolutely no independent evidence for the existence of another census twenty-eight years after that taken by Quirinius on the deposition of Archelaus.

Summary

The evidence has led us to the four years of **33 to 36** CE as those possible for the crucifixion of Jesus, with the possibility that this could be reduced if Schonfield is correct about the later census. It is also interesting to note that if we could confidently assign the single year of 6 CE, the actual year of the deposition of Archelaus, to the census of Quirinius we could reduce the range for Jesus' crucifixion to the two years 35 and 36 CE. I shall leave it to others to decide if the lack of proof for the continuation of censuses at fourteen-year intervals is sufficient to exclude Schonfield's hypothesis or not.

I believe that this is the best that can be achieved in dating the year of Jesus' crucifixion without resorting to surmise, predilection or faith. That we have also been able to reduce the range of years allowable for both the nativity and the beginning of his public life has been an unexpected bonus.

It is time to summarize what this investigation has discovered.

Stained glass from the church of Saint-Ours, Loches, France

3

The chronology

A matter of fact

Below is the chronology of all the key events that we have derived, together with the dates of other, related events. Those highlighted are derived directly from the references in the Gospels.

Event	Most probable dates
The birth of Jesus	10 to 7 BCE
The beginning of Jesus' public life at Bethania	22 to 26 CE
The first Passover of Jesus' public life	23 to 26 CE
The baptism at Aenon	26 to 29 CE
The arrest of John	27 to 29 CE
The death of John the Baptist	27 to 35 CE
The 'not yet 50' rebuke	32 to 35 CE
The crucifixion of Jesus	33 to 36 CE

The range of dates we have for Jesus' birth excludes the possibility of his having been born during the year of the Quirinian census that was taken on the deposition of Archelaus. However, this does not prove that there was an earlier census that history has forgotten, nor does it prove that this association was caused by Jesus having been in Jerusalem in that year for his 'coming of age' on the attainment of his 13th year.

There are three events that are still absent from this summary: the baptism of Jesus by John, the temptation in the wilderness and the beginning of Jesus' ministry.

The baptism I have omitted because I have reservations about its authenticity, as I have explained before. But if it did occur then we would have to include it where, and when, the Synoptists suggest: at Bethania, immediately before the 'dove incident'.

The temptation I have omitted because the order of events found in Luke, together with the redefining of the other related evidence he provides, now allows this event to have occurred at almost any time between the baptism at Bethania and just after the baptism at Aenon (that is, in the period from 22 to 29 CE). We therefore cannot position it reliably in the sequence of events.

The beginning of Jesus' ministry suffers from a similar fate. Although we now know that it began in one of the years 23 to 26 CE, it still cannot be positioned in the sequence of events with any degree of certainty. What we can say, however, is that the evidence, when considered as a whole, makes it clear that the start of the ministry is not a simple thing to define. There might even have been a 'false start' followed by a period when Jesus retreated back into obscurity before relaunching himself for the final phase of his mission.

From the above we can see that the time span from the beginning of Jesus' public life at Bethania to his crucifixion at Golgotha was between just under fifteen years and just over six. Even at its shortest, this is considerably longer than is assumed in Christian tradition. Nevertheless I find myself in surprisingly exalted company here, as none other than Iranaeus believed that Jesus' ministry could have lasted for fifteen years.

I have now completed what I set out to achieve: a chronology for the life of Jesus that considers and allows for the accommodation of every piece of chronological evidence that resides within the four Gospels. In doing this I believe I have shown transparency of process and fidelity to the chronology of the historical background. I hope I have not allowed prejudice, in the literal sense of the word, to take precedence over the historical fact, reason or logic. Whether I have succeeded in accurately deriving the real chronology for the life of Jesus should now be purely dependent on the accuracy of the evidence.

Table 4 shows the relationship between the historical timeline and all dateable events recorded in the Four Canonical Gospels of the New Testament.

Stained glass from the church of Saint-Pierre, Dreux, France

Table 4

Historical event			AUC	BCE/CE
	Possible years for the accession *de jure* of Herod the Great		714	40
			715	39
			716	38
			717	37
			718	36
			719	35
			720	34
			721	33
			722	32
			723	31
			724	30
			725	29
			726	28
			727	27
			728	26
			729	25
			730	24
			731	23
	Possible years for beginning of the temple rebuild by Herod the Great		732	22
			733	21
			734	20
			735	19
			736	18
			737	17
			738	16
			739	15
			740	14
			741	13
Consular year of Quirinius		Year of Halley's comet	742	12
Whereabouts of Quirinius unknown			743	11

Table 4 continued

Historical events			AUC	BCE/CE
Years for which the whereabouts of Quirinius are unknown or uncertain			744	10
			745	9
			746	8
	Execution of Herod the Great's Hasmodean sons	Three conjunctions in Pisces	747	7
		Possible triple conjunction	748	6
		Year of the nova	749	5
	Death of Herod the Great	Lunar eclipse in Judaea	750	4
			751	3
			752	2
			753	1 BCE
			754	1 CE
			755	2
			756	3
			757	4
	Possible years for census of Quirinius		758	5
		Archelaus deposed	759	6
			760	7
			761	8
			762	9
			763	10
			764	11
			765	12
	Tiberius co-Emperor of Rome		766	13
	Tiberius sole Emperor of Rome		767	14
			768	15
			769	16
			770	17
			771	18

Biblical events			
Possible years for the birth of Jesus			
Possible years for Jesus to have been in his 13th year (12 years old)			

Table 4 continued

		Historical events	AUC	CE
			772	19
			773	20
			774	21
			775	22
		Possible years for '46 years since temple rebuild began' riposte	776	23
			777	24
			778	25
			779	26
The years of the governorship of Judaea under Pontius Pilate		Possible years for '15th year' of reign of Tiberius	780	27
			781	28
			782	29
			783	30
			784	31
			785	32
			786	33
			787	34
			788	35
			789	36

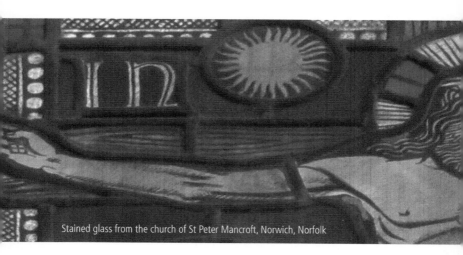

Stained glass from the church of St Peter Mancroft, Norwich, Norfolk

Biblical events			
Jesus 'about 30' if born in years 10 to 7 BCE	Possible years for beginning of Jesus' public life	Possible years for first Passover of Jesus' public life	Possible years for baptisms at Bethania
		Possible years of John's arrest	Possible years for baptisms at Aenon
Possible years for execution of Jesus	Possible years for 'not yet 50' rebuke		

What follows is very much:

A matter of opinion

I am now about to indulge myself by breaking some of the rules that formed the framework of this investigation. I am about to select dates from ranges in order to suggest a chronology and an interpretation of events for which there is some evidence, but no real proof. I believe that my reasoning is sound, but I accept that some of the information on which it is based is not universally accepted as reliable fact. Nevertheless, during this investigation, I found myself being drawn in a certain direction that seems to provide a better and more complete explanation of the Gospel evidence than does the traditional consensus-based narrative. It is based on logic and the belief that the truth is distinctly Jewish.

The basis of this logic not only rests on, but is, I believe, required by the significance of age, the Feast of the Passover, and the Temple, in Jewish life at that time. This is what the result of this proposal leads me to believe could be close to the truth.

Event	Most probable dates
The birth of John the Baptist	12–8 BCE
Earliest time for Jesus' birth: from immediately after the Passover of	8 BCE
Latest time for the birth of Jesus: until and including the Passover of	7 BCE
Herod the Great executes his Hasmodean sons, and Joseph leaves Bethlehem and takes his family to Egypt, later in the same year	7 BCE
On hearing of Herod's death Joseph takes his family to live in Galilee, being afraid to return to Bethlehem, because of Archelaus's accession	4 BCE

Jesus in Jerusalem, at Passover, for his coming of age, at 12 years old, in the most likely year for the census of Quirinius	6 CE
John the Baptist proclaims Jesus, who then begins his public life, at Bethania, at the age of 30	23 or 24 CE
Jesus and Mary Magdalene marry at Cana-in-Galilee	24 CE
The first Passover of his public life, 46 (elapsed) years after the rebuilding of the Temple began, also at the age of 30	24 CE
The 'wilderness years': a period of time of which we know very little about his activities: between the years	24 to 28 CE
Jesus reappears with his disciples at Aenon, near to where John is also baptising followers, and there is a dispute between their disciples	28 CE
John is arrested at Aenon, after which Jesus' campaign begins in earnest	28 CE
The death of John	28 to 35 CE
The 'not yet 50' rebuke (when Jesus is 41 or 42 years old)	34 or 35 CE
The crucifixion of Jesus (at 42 or 43 years old)	35 or 36 CE

The ages of twelve and thirty are believed to have been significant landmarks: the former as a rite of passage to adulthood, and the latter as the beginning of the age of authority, which I believe is particularly significant if Jesus was a rabbi, as is frequently stated in the Gospels. Although it was not until 70 CE, when the Temple was destroyed, that rabbinic Judaism replaced Temple-based Judaism, there is a body of belief that a form of rabbinic Judaism existed before the sacking of Jerusalem. This seems highly likely to have been the case among those Jews for whom distance and circumstance had combined to deny them ready access to the Temple. There is also a strong body of belief that this early form originated in Galilee, which would have made Jesus a rabbi in the tradition of the hasidim and not a post-70 CE midrash rabbi, as we still have today. The difference is somewhat akin to that between a sage/teacher and a vicar, as I understand it.

So I began with the idea suggested by the second of the two-nativities hypotheses, that Jesus was in Jerusalem for Passover at the age of 12, as part of the celebration of his coming of age, and that this occurred in the year of the census of Quirinius. Until now I have allowed for the three years 5 to 7 CE for this event, but as I explained in the Nativity section, I strongly believe that the actual year for this was 6 CE. This explains the two references from Josephus that this occurred in both the ninth year and the tenth year of Archelaus' reign, as 6 CE is made up of the last part of the former and the first part of the latter. Now, for Jesus to have been 12 years of age at the Passover of this year he must have been born after the Passover of 8 BCE and before the Passover of 7 BCE.

Next I considered the likelihood that the proclamation of Jesus as 'the lamb of God' by John the Baptist and the subsequent beginning of his public life at Bethania occurred after the dove incident when he was 30 years of age. Certainly he could not have been younger than 30 at Bethania, as he was being addressed as rabbi at that time. It is believed that 30 was the qualifying age for this status. Working forwards, from the interval we now have for his birth to his 30th birthday, takes us to the interval between the ends of the Passovers of 23 and 24 CE. From the information already derived we find that the year 22 CE is the earliest year allowable for the baptisms at Bethania, and the year 23 CE is the earliest year for the first Passover of Jesus' public life. This allows for two possible ways in which Jesus was 30 years old when he was proclaimed by John at Bethania and when he was at the Temple for the first Passover of his public life. Both require the Passover of 24 CE to be the first Passover, but it is still possible for his 30th birthday and Bethania to have been either late in 776/23 or early in 24 CE.

This, in its turn, requires that the 'not yet 50 rebuke' was made either late in 34 CE, when Jesus was 41, or late in 35 CE, when he was either 41 or 42, and it places the crucifixion at the Passover of either 35 or 36 CE, when he was either 41 or 42 respectively. I have to admit that I favour the year 36 CE, as the year of his execution, for no other reason than, like Hugh Schonfield, I cannot help wanting Jesus' crucifixion to have somehow been related both to Pilate's recall to Rome and to the overthrowing of Caiaphas as high priest. But I accept that this is a preference, not a fact.

I find it frustrating that, although this hypothesis suggests a time span of only twelve months within which Jesus was born, we cannot resolve the time of his execution to a single year. Nevertheless, this chronology represents a much more complete version of a 'reality' that is both possible and honest. I think it takes proper consideration of the problems and contradictions. This hypothesis might be wrong, and it is certainly unproven. But it fits everything that we know.

tained glass from the church of Saint-Etienne, Villandry, France

Stained glass from the church of Saint-Pierre, Dreux, France

References

Note: Wikipedia sources are given at some points in the text, but are not listed here. Where Wikipedia was used as a source, the information was always checked independently.

Appian (c. 160 CE) *Historia Romana*. English translation of part available online at: www.livius.org/ap-ark/appian/appian_illyrian_00.html (last accessed 18 April 2013).

Ashgrove (nd) 'Triple conjunction of Jupiter and Saturn', www.public.iastate.edu/~lightandlife/triple.htm (last accessed 18 April 2013).

Astrosurf (2010) 'Some notes on the visibility of the 5 BC Chinese star', www.astrosurf.com/comets/cometas/Star/Visibility_Star.htm (last accessed 18 April 2013).

Augustus Caesar (14 CE/1998) *Res Gesta Divi Augusti* (The Deeds of the Divine Augustus), trans. Thomas Bushnell. Available online at: http://classics.mit.edu/Augustus/deeds.html (last accessed 18 April 2013).

Baigent, Michael and Leigh, Richard (1991) *The Dead Sea Scrolls Deception*. New York: Simon & Schuster.

Berger, Klaus (2011) *Kommentar Zum Neuen Testament*, 2nd edn. Munich, Germany: Gütersloher Verlagshaus.

Burgess, Anthony (1982) *Man of Nazareth*. New York: Bantam.

Carrier, Richard (2006) 'Luke vs. Matthew on the year of Christ's birth.' Available online at: www.errancywiki.com/index.php?title= Legends&rcid=41896 (last accessed 18 April 2013).

Consuls, Roman, list of. Available online at: www.roman-empire.net/articles/article-024.html (last accessed 18 April 2013).

Dawkins, Richard (2006) *The God Delusion*. New York: Houghton Mifflin Harcourt.

Dio, Cassius (c. 200 CE) *Historia Romana*. English translation of part available online at: http://penelope.uchicago.edu/Thayer/E/Roman/Texts/Cassius_Dio/(last accessed 18 April 2013).

Josephus, Flavius (c. 78 CE) *The Jewish Wars*. Available online at: www.biblestudytools.com/history/flavius-josephus/war-of-the-jews/ (last accessed 18 April 2013).

Josephus, Flavius (c. 94 CE) *Antiquities of the Jews*. Available online at: www.gutenberg.org/files/2848/2848-h/2848-h.htm (last accessed 18 April 2013).

Loisy, Alfred Firmin (1902) *L'Évangile et l'Église*. Paris: Picard.

English edn as *The Gospel and the Church*, Philadelphia, Pa.: Fortress (1976).

New Advent Catholic Encyclopaedia. www.newadvent.org/cathen/ (last accessed 18 April 2013).

New English Bible. Available online at: http://www.biblegateway.com/blog/2012/11/the-new-english-translation-net-bible-is-here/

Parpola, Simo (2001) 'The magi and the star', *Bible Review*, **17**(6) (December): 16–23, 52–4.

Patrizi, Francis Xavier (1853) *De Evangeliis*, 3 vols. Freiburg im Breisgau, Germany: Verlag Herder.

Ratzinger, Joseph (2012) *Jesus of Nazareth: The infancy narratives.* Colorado Springs, Colo.: Image Books.

Schonfield, Hugh (1965) *The Passover Plot: New light on the history of Jesus.* New York: Bernard Geis Associates.

Suetonius (121 CE/2011) *Lives of the Twelve Caesars*, trans. Donna W. Hurley. Indianapolis, Ind./London: Hackett.

Thiering, Barbara (1993) *Jesus the Man: New interpretation from the Dead Sea Scrolls.* New York; Transworld.

Zeffirelli, Franco (1977) *Jesus of Nazareth*, television series.

Stained glass from the Sainte Chapelle at Champigny-sur-Veude, France

Index

Stained glass from the church of Notre Dame, Beaufort-en-Vallée, France

Also published by the Lasse Press

An illustrated biography of William de la Pole, first duke of Suffolk (1396–1450)

William de la Pole spent half his life fighting for the Lancastrian kings in France, in the later stages of the Hundred Years War. The war cost him his father and his four brothers. Taken prisoner, he lost a fortune paying his ransom – and gained two friends: his captor, the bastard of Orleans, and the bastard's half-brother, the famous French poet Charles of Orleans. Suffolk, also a poet, was to become Orleans' jailer. He spent the remainder of his life trying to bring about peace between England and France. It made him the most hated man in England.

This powerful true story of friendship, loyalty and treachery is the first full-length biography of an extraordinary man. Susan Curran uses a wide range of sources including contemporary documents and chronicles to bring Suffolk's story to life. The illustrations include photographs of the places Suffolk knew, and many stunning examples of contemporary stained glass from England and France.

Susan Curran has been a professional writer and publisher for more than 30 years. This is her first biography.

First published 2011
ISBN-13: 978-0-9568758-0-8 (large-format paperback)
Also available in a range of electronic editions

For more information on all Lasse Press books, visit

www.lassepress.com

Published by the Lasse Press in October 2013

A true story of two lovers in medieval East Anglia

When Margery Paston announced that she wished to marry her family's land agent, Richard Calle, her mother and her brothers resisted the idea so strongly that rather than let her follow her heart, they created a public feud.

One of her brothers wrote that Richard Calle 'should never have my goodwill to make my sister sell candles and mustard at Framlingham'. True, Richard's family ran a shop: but Richard was an intelligent, well-educated professional man, perfectly capable of keeping a wife in the manner that might have been expected of Margery's husband. So why were her family so determined to prevent the marriage? Was it really because they believed it was socially beneath them, or were there other hidden reasons?

The Paston letters are well known as an unique source of knowledge about an English family in the fifteenth century. They form the main source for this account of Richard and Margery's lives, which also draws on many other sources, including the author's first-hand knowledge of the places the Pastons knew and lived in.

The book is illustrated in colour throughout, with maps, family trees and photographs of East Anglian scenes and medieval stained glass.

ISBN-13: 978-0-9568758-4-6 (large-format paperback)
Also available in a Kindle edition

For more information on all Lasse Press books, visit

www.lassepress.com